LINN SJÖBERG

THE SWEDISH DEATH CLEANING

Bible

3 Books in 1

The Complete Guide to Quickly Organize and Declutter Your Spaces for Happier Living

Table of Contents

INTRODUCTION

Welcome, dear reader, to *"The Swedish Death Cleaning Bible"*. This is not just a book, but a gentle invitation into a life-changing journey – a journey that weaves together the heartening philosophy of Swedish Death Cleaning with real, hands-on strategies to breathe fresh air into your life. This lovingly crafted guide, divided into three thoughtful sections, unfolds a world where decluttering is not a chore, but a heartwarming process of liberation and self-discovery. In these pages, you will find more than advice; you'll uncover a pathway to tranquility, simplicity, and an uncluttered life filled with joy and serenity.

Book I delves into the philosophy of Swedish Death Cleaning, a method that seamlessly intertwines the concepts of mindful living and mortality. You'll learn about the foundational principles of this holistic approach, understand its cultural significance, and see how it differs from other decluttering methods. Furthermore, we'll explore the impacts of this practice on mental well-being and how it enhances mindfulness, intentional living, relationships, and personal legacy.

Book II offers step-by-step guidance on implementing Swedish Death Cleaning in your own life. From assessing your readiness to setting clear goals and creating a realistic timeline, we'll provide a detailed look at the entire process. Unique Swedish strategies for sorting, discarding, organizing items will be discussed along with addressing digital clutter with proven techniques inspired by Swedish minimalism. Finally, maintaining a clutter-free space will be achieved by adopting Swedish principles and building sustainable habits.

Book III focuses on the emotional journey connected to Swedish Death Cleaning. As your surroundings transform so too will your emotions.

Navigating emotional resistance, attachment and guilt are necessary obstacles to overcome on this journey. The emotional experience also encompasses deeper self-discovery and reflection –unearthing personal narratives and exploring life changes through the lens of Swedish Death Cleaning. Lastly, we will address mortality acceptance and letting go while embracing decluttering as a liberating way to face our ultimate fate.

Prepare to delve into the transformative world of Swedish Death Cleaning. I hope you will find solace and a renewed sense of calm through these pages, like a comforting, sweet cinnamon bun fresh out of the oven. We will whisper wisdom about life's ever-changing tides, reminding you, dear one, of life's impermanence and how we can find peace within it. Together, we will learn to cherish the fleeting moments of joy and sorrow, tidying our spaces and hearts, while quietly preparing for what may come next. Embrace the Swedish-inspired lifestyle, a way of living filled with love, simplicity, and mindful acceptance.

Have a good read,

Linn Sjöberg

BOOK 1: EMBRACING THE PHILOSOPHY

UNDERSTANDING SWEDISH DEATH CLEANING

In this chapter, we embark on an enlightening journey to explore and understand the intriguing and practical tradition called *"Swedish Death Cleaning."* First, we shall delve into its definition, origins, and the cultural significance that this remarkable practice holds in Scandinavian societies. The power of Swedish Death Cleaning resides not only in its tangible effects but also in the profound philosophy that guides it, shaping one's perspective on material possessions and life itself.

As we delve deeper into the unique philosophy behind Swedish Death Cleaning, we will uncover why it has garnered attention around the globe over recent years. We shall compare this practice with general decluttering methods, highlighting its distinct features that set it apart from other organizational techniques. Understanding how Swedish Death Cleaning transcends common decluttering practices will give you a deeper appreciation for its transformative potential.

DEFINITION, ORIGINS AND CULTURAL SIGNIFICANCE

Life is often filled with unnecessary clutter. We accumulate possessions that eventually end up stacked away in corners or buried in boxes, forgotten and collecting dust. As we grow older, the thought of leaving this chaos behind for our loved ones to deal with becomes a growing concern. Swedish Death

Cleaning, or "*döstädning*" in Swedish, is a thoughtful and practical approach to decluttering and organizing one's life to make it easier for those left behind.

Swedish Death Cleaning is a unique cultural tradition that has gained popularity recently as more people seek ways to simplify their lives and make their home environments less chaotic. It is a gentle and purposeful method of organizing your belongings and deciding what you genuinely need to keep and what can be given away or discarded.

One of the key principles of Swedish Death Cleaning is coming to terms with one's mortality while simultaneously reflecting on the value of personal belongings. By acknowledging that no one lives forever, we can begin to minimize the clutter surrounding us, which ultimately helps our loved ones manage our remains without feeling overwhelmed.

Practicing Swedish Death Cleaning means examining every object in your home and assessing its worthwhile considering others' needs. Memories are cherished elements of life, but they don't require a physical presence. Photos or written letters could replace sentimental items so your loved ones can remember you through mementos without being weighed down by excessive possessions.

Moreover, Swedish Death Cleaning encourages open communication with friends and family about your wishes. As you declutter and organize, involving loved ones eases future burdens and strengthens bonds through shared experiences and memories. This inherent transparency provides peace of mind to all parties involved.

To practice Swedish Death Cleaning, focus on one room or area in your home. Organize belongings into three categories: keep, give away, and discard. While deciding an item's fate, ask yourself questions like, "Do I need this?", "Have I used it recently?", "Will it bring joy to someone else?", or "Is it time to let it go?". Once you sort through each category, give away or discard the items promptly. Don't be shy to involve loved ones in this process, as they may appreciate items with personal significance or memories attached.

Swedish Death Cleaning is not exclusively for the elderly or terminally ill; it is an ongoing process that can benefit individuals at any stage of life. By routinely decluttering and streamlining possessions throughout life, Swedish Death Cleaning fosters a sense of mindfulness towards material possessions – helping us focus on cherished memories rather than getting bogged down by physical clutter.

Ultimately, the purpose of Swedish Death Cleaning is to make our lives and the lives of those we leave behind more comfortable and peaceful. It is an act of love that revolves around respect and thoughtfulness for our loved ones whom we entrust with handling our affairs when the time comes. This mindful cleaning process offers us solace while keeping life's memories alive without letting material clutter dictate our existence. Embracing Swedish Death Cleaning teaches us that even in death, we can continue to care for those we love by leaving them a simplified space filled with cherished memories instead of unnecessary belongings.

Origins

Swedish Death Cleaning, or "döstädning," traces its origins to Scandinavian households' longstanding traditions and practices. The term itself is a combination of two Swedish words, "dö" (death) and "städning" (cleaning), which encapsulates the essence of this unique practice.

Historically, Sweden has long embraced the importance of cleanliness and order. The country's notoriously harsh winters compelled residents to maintain tidy homes that could withstand the forces of nature. Moreover, close-knit communities meant that one's household organization could reflect onto their reputation and relationships with neighbors.

Over time, the broader Scandinavian ethos developed around these values, emphasizing frugality, pragmatism, and self-sufficiency. This cultural context provided the perfect backdrop for döstädning to emerge as a common practice in Sweden.

The Swedish Death Cleaning movement gained momentum in the 20th century as societal attitudes shifted toward more eco-friendly lifestyles and sustainable living practices. With a focus on minimizing waste while maximizing utility, this trend resonated with Swedes who sought to achieve a greater sense of order and purpose.

At its core, döstädning serves as a means of decluttering one's home to prepare for life's final stages or when one passes away. This process involves sorting through possessions accumulated throughout one's lifetime and determining what will be kept, discarded, donated, or given to family members and friends.

Swedish Death Cleaning gained international attention when Margareta Magnusson wrote "The Gentle Art of Swedish Death Cleaning" in 2017. The book introduced this Scandinavian practice to global audiences searching for productive and mindful ways to deal with mortality while creating a well-organized living space.

Through her writing, Margareta has inspired individuals worldwide to consider their mortality and acknowledge that leaving behind an organized home can be an act of love for surviving family members. The Swedish Death Cleaning movement now transcends borders, appealing to people of various cultures who recognize that tackling clutter and discussing end-of-life decisions can foster deeper connections with loved ones.

Today, döstädning continues to generate interest and intrigue as it teaches valuable lessons on living simply, embracing mortality, and creating a loving legacy for those we leave behind. The history of Swedish Death Cleaning reminds us that practicality and mindfulness can coexist harmoniously in our quest for a meaningful life.

Cultural Significance

Sweden, a land of timeless beauty and deeply entrenched cultural practices, boasts a unique custom called "döstädning" - death cleaning. Transcending the confines of regular housekeeping, this practice holds immense cultural significance in the country, shaping and enhancing the lives of individuals and families.

The cultural significance of döstädning lies in its core values— mindfulness, simplicity, and selflessness. By organizing one's belongings and considering what truly matters in life, Swedes demonstrate their intimate connection with values that stand the test of time. Death cleaning becomes more than tidying up; it transforms into an art form incorporating reflection and contemplation.

Mindfulness is imperative as one embarks on the path of döstädning. It requires attention to each item's emotional weight while deciding what stays and what goes. In doing so, people acknowledge the inherent memories attached to their possessions while detaching themselves from unnecessary clutter.

Simplicity fuels the practice, urging individuals to prioritize quality relationships over material wealth. This shift in focus leads Swedes to choose experiences over excess; less becomes more. The notion of living with only what adds value strengthens the bond between family members as they collectively navigate through losses or changes that life throws at them.

But at its heart is *selflessness* - this is where Swedish death cleaning truly stands out as a culturally significant practice. By tidying up one's life systematically, people ensure that their loved ones are not burdened with the task later. This powerful act of love unifies families and fosters intimacy; it acknowledges that life is fleeting and the people who matter most take center stage.

The Swedish death cleaning process educates us on the importance of leaving a legacy. It empowers individuals to decide how they want their lives remembered while allowing them control over the narrative. Preserving memories through photographs, letters, and carefully curated belongings sustains individuality and allows precious stories to be passed on for generations.

As döstädning gains global recognition, it provokes reflection on the contemporary consumer culture that promotes mindless accumulation. The Swedish practice illuminates the stark contrast between our current values and the more sustainable living ethos practiced elsewhere.

In conclusion, Swedish death cleaning is a powerful cultural practice that teaches us valuable lessons about living intentionally while focusing on what truly matters. Its essence is mindfulness, simplicity, and selflessness - core values that resonate across generations and time. As we embrace this age-old wisdom from a distant land, we embark on a journey of self-discovery that liberates us from our possessions and embraces a more holistic approach to life—one where peace, harmony, and meaningful relationships find space to flourish.

THE UNIQUE PHILOSOPHY BEHIND SDC

Once you become familiar with Swedish death cleaning, it's easy to see that there is more to it than simply decluttering a home. At its heart lies a distinct philosophy combining mindfulness, responsibility, and practicality, resulting in a transformative process allowing easier navigation through life. In this section, we will explore the unique principles that form the core of Swedish death cleaning and discover how they can lead us toward a more meaningful existence.

1. Acknowledging the Inevitability of Death: Most people prefer not to think about their mortality. However, in the philosophy of Swedish death cleaning, acknowledging death is a crucial first step. By accepting the inevitable nature of one's passing, individuals can free themselves from the overwhelming burden of material possessions they accumulate throughout their lives. This mindset provides motivation and purpose in organizing and decluttering one's living space.

2. Taking Responsibility for Your Impact: Secondly, embracing Swedish death cleaning involves taking responsibility for how your actions affect others around you – primarily your loved ones left behind after your passing. By decluttering your home and removing unnecessary belongings, you make their lives easier as they have fewer items to sort through, making decisions about what to keep or discard more manageable. This act of kindness alleviates emotional stress during an already challenging time.

3. Foster Mindful Connections with Objects: The philosophy behind Swedish death cleaning prompts individuals to examine their emotional attachments to possessions with greater scrutiny. Instead of blindly clinging to objects for sentimental reasons or out of habit, this practice asks people to consider whether their belongings still serve a purpose or bring joy. If an object fails this test, it may be time to find a new home or be given away.

4. Prioritize Quality Over Quantity: A key component of Swedish death cleaning is shifting focus from quantity to quality regarding the possessions one accumulates. Mindful owners of well-made, durable objects usually feel more satisfied and fulfilled than those who own numerous, low-quality items. Therefore, it is crucial to consider the value and potential longevity of each item purchased from here on out. This approach ultimately leads to a more purposeful and lasting connection with your belongings.

5. Simplify Life Through Decluttering: Decluttering is not just about material possessions; it's also about simplifying one's life. Our environments significantly impact our mental health, with clutter often leading to feelings of anxiety and stress. By embracing a minimalist lifestyle through Swedish death cleaning, one may find greater peace of mind and improved overall well-being due to the cleaner, uncluttered space.

6. Encouraging Generosity: Swedish death cleaning also fosters a sense of generosity in those who practice it. Throughout this process, you will likely find many items that no longer serve a functional or emotional purpose for you but may benefit someone else's life. Donating these belongings to charitable organizations or giving them away to friends or family members furthers the spirit of generosity that runs deep within the core of this philosophy.

7. Commemorating Memories Rather Than Holding Onto Items: Swedish death cleaning encourages individuals to let go of attachment to material possessions by finding alternative ways to commemorate important moments or cherished memories. Instead of clinging onto objects for their emotional significance, one can create photo albums, write memoirs, or develop creative projects that epitomize memories while maintaining a streamlined living environment.

In summary, the unique philosophy behind Swedish death cleaning goes far beyond mere decluttering – it imparts a comprehensive shift in how we perceive our belongings and relationships with others. We can transition into a more fulfilling existence by cultivating mindfulness, personal responsibility, practicality, and simplicity in our daily lives. As you delve deeper into the practice of Swedish death cleaning, consider how these principles can reshape your perspective and provide a clear path towards a more meaningful life.

HOW SDC DIFFERS FROM OTHER DECLUTTERING METHODS

Swedish Death Cleaning differs significantly from other general decluttering methods, such as the KonMari method, minimalist decluttering, and the four-box method, to name a few. The primary factor sets Swedish Death Cleaning apart from these other strategies is its purpose and philosophy.

The main objective of Swedish Death Cleaning is not simply to declutter, but rather to lessen the burden on loved ones after one's passing by curating a more manageable and meaningful collection of possessions. This idea stems from the belief that leaving an excess of belongings to family members to sort through during the grieving process is unfair. Individuals actively take responsibility for their possessions by engaging in this practice and leaving a purposeful and cherished legacy behind.

To better understand how Swedish Death Cleaning differs from general decluttering methods, it is necessary to examine some key distinctions in philosophy, mindset, tactics, and timeline:

1. Philosophy and Mindset: While most decluttering methods focus on enhancing one's life through organization and the satisfaction derived from a tidy space, Swedish Death Cleaning takes a more generous approach. It is centered around empathy for loved ones who will be impacted by our belongings posthumously. This tactic encourages individuals not only to assess the physical aspects of their belongings but also to evaluate their emotional significance.

2. Incremental vs. Drastic Change: Unlike some decluttering methods which emphasize quick and drastic changes to transform one's space (such as the KonMari method), Swedish Death Cleaning advocates for an incremental process. This technique allows for a more thorough evaluation of possessions while preventing overwhelm during decluttering.

3. Prioritizing Sentimental Items: Most general decluttering methods employ criteria such as utility, necessity, and joy to determine which items to keep or discard. Contrarily, Swedish Death Cleaning places a stronger emphasis on the sentimental value of possessions. Practitioners are encouraged to consider if the item holds meaning to them, and if so, whether it would bring the same sense of importance and enjoyment to their loved ones.

4. Open Communication: A distinct feature of Swedish Death Cleaning is promoting open dialogue with family members about their possessions and how they will be managed after one's passing. This reflection creates an opportunity for meaningful conversations among loved ones on topics such as inheritance, memory sharing, and family history.

5. Timeline: Unlike general decluttering methods which may be employed at any point in one's life with no definitive end-point, Swedish Death Cleaning emphasizes a long-term approach with a clear purpose. Ideally, it should begin in middle age and continue throughout one's lifetime so that individuals can consistently reassess their possessions and their legacy.

6. Emphasis on Social Responsibility: Besides considering the impact on loved ones, Swedish Death Cleaning also highlights social responsibility through donation and recycling options for discarded belongings. This emphasizes environmental consciousness and encourages practitioners to think critically about how their possessions will impact society even after departure.

7. Memento Choice: The process of selecting mementos to keep during the Swedish Death Cleaning process differs from methods like KonMari wherein items must "spark joy." In this method, individuals are encouraged to retain possessions that tell a story or hold a connection to deceased loved ones or essential life events.

In conclusion, Swedish Death Cleaning is an altruistically driven decluttering method that focuses on easing the burdens placed on future generations by thoughtfully curating personal belongings for a meaningful legacy. Its unique distinctions in philosophy, mindset, tactics, communication, incremental progress, social responsibility, and long-term timeline set it apart from general decluttering methods commonly utilized today. By incorporating the principles of Swedish Death Cleaning, individuals can achieve not only a decluttered and organized space but also the gratification in knowing they have eased the emotional load for their loved ones, created space for cherished memories, and contributed to a more ecologically responsible society.

THE IMPACTS OF SWEDISH DEATH CLEANING

This chapter delves into the transformative world of Swedish Death Cleaning, a practice that simplifies our surroundings and holds the key to a more fulfilling life. With its roots in the Scandinavian concept of "döstädning," we explore how this method goes beyond simple decluttering and into mental well-being, mindfulness, and intentional living.

We unveil the intricate connection between our physical possessions and mental health, becoming increasingly aware of how our cluttered spaces echo within our minds. From this realization, we showcase how Swedish Death Cleaning helps nurture a sense of mindfulness and intent in how we live, allowing us to take control of our lives by connecting deeply and meaningfully with each item we own.

As we commence this enlightening journey, you will discover this practice's profound impact on your relationships, lifestyle, and legacy. Embrace stronger connections with your loved ones, renewed vigor in your daily activities, and ultimately align yourself with a powerful sense of purpose—all through the enlightening art of Swedish Death Cleaning.

PHYSICAL CLUTTER AND MENTAL WELL-BEING

The premise behind Swedish death cleaning is that physical clutter creates an unnecessary burden on the individual and their loved ones. By systematically sorting through and removing excess possessions, we can free up space in our homes and minds for better mental well-being.

The term 'death cleaning' might sound morbid, but it isn't meant to be negative or focus solely on mortality. Rather, it's about examining the material possessions we've accumulated over our lives and deciding what truly holds value for us while making conscious choices regarding what to keep and let go. This mindful approach to decluttering has been praised for promoting emotional and mental balance, allowing individuals to live more enriched lives with less anxiety and stress.

One significant connection between physical clutter and mental well-being is the proven link between cluttered environments and stress levels. Stress is a natural human response that helps us cope with challenging situations. However, constant exposure to disorganized surroundings can trigger chronic stress responses that harm our mental health. Studies have shown that living in cluttered spaces can lead to increased cortisol levels—the primary stress hormone produced by the body—and feelings of anxiety, depression, and even relationship issues.

Consequently, Swedish death cleaning helps relieve this constant state of hyperarousal by creating a more serene and harmonious living environment. As individuals sort through their possessions, they free up physical space and release the psychological load of owning too many things. By prioritizing belongings based on personal meaning and utility, participants learn to appreciate what they have and let go of items that no longer serve them while reducing feelings of overwhelming mental burden.

Another connection between physical clutter and mental well-being relates to the phenomenon known as *'clutter blindness.'* Clutter blindness occurs when individuals become so used to their chaotic surroundings that they fail to recognize the detrimental effects on their mental health. For many, Swedish death cleaning acts as a catalyst, illuminating the excessive number of possessions that may hinder personal growth and happiness. This newfound awareness helps individuals understand the importance of decluttering and fosters a conscious pursuit of minimalism that benefits mental well-being.

Moreover, Swedish death cleaning encourages open communication among family members, helping to address unresolved emotions and promote deeper relationships. As people discuss the fate of certain possessions, they can share memories, laughter, and even tears, facilitating a path for healing and emotional growth. In this way, decluttering is not just removing physical items from the home but also a personal journey through self-reflection and discovery. Identifying what is truly important in our lives, we reconnect with our values, improving overall life satisfaction and well-being.

Additionally, Swedish death cleaning fosters independence and self-sufficiency in older adults while mitigating caregiver stress. By proactively addressing their clutter, seniors reduce the burden on loved ones who may otherwise be responsible for sorting through their belongings after they pass away. This preparedness affirms older adults' autonomy while providing peace of mind for family members.

In conclusion, Swedish death cleaning is not solely about organizing physical spaces; it is a reflective process with far-reaching implications on mental well-being. Decluttering allows for more focused thoughts, reduced stress, and increased emotional resilience. Through communication and self-reflection by Swedish death cleaning, individuals are empowered to live purposefully while unencumbered by unnecessary possessions. This practice serves as a reminder that creating balance within our environment—both physically and mentally—can lead to more meaningful, healthy, and fulfilling lives.

How SDC Enhances Intentional Living

Death is an inevitable part of life, and the concept of mortality has been a topic of contemplation by countless philosophers and poets throughout the ages. If we shift our perspective to view death as a transformative process, it can provide us with valuable insights into the meaning of life itself. This is where Swedish death cleaning comes into play – it's a practice that deals with the practical aspects of decluttering one's possessions and encompasses a profound spiritual awakening.

Swedish death cleaning is a decluttering process that encourages individuals to mindfully reevaluate the material items in their lives – stripping away the excess baggage to focus on what truly matters.

By engaging in Swedish death cleaning, we can cultivate *mindfulness* within our daily lives. Mindfulness is the practice of being consciously aware of and present in each moment instead of being caught up in the whirlwind of distractions and struggles that often pervade our modern existence.

As we begin the journey of Swedish death cleaning, we must confront our attachments to material possessions. We can learn to detach ourselves from more than just physical clutter by assessing each item and questioning its value in our lives. This process requires a deep introspection regarding our priorities and values – examining what truly adds meaning to our existence.

Through this examination, we can recognize how much of our lives are occupied by external distractions or the pursuit of material wealth. As we shed these unnecessary distractions, focusing on what enriches our lives becomes easier – prioritizing relationships, experiences, and self-improvement over materialism.

As a result of this paradigm shift, *intentional living* is cultivated. Intentional living means embracing every aspect of your life with purpose, from the objects in your home to the relationships you nurture. As we undertake Swedish death cleaning, we choose what to keep and what to release, allowing for more clarity and direction in living a life aligned with our values.

The process of Swedish death cleaning also highlights the way material possessions can carry emotional weight – a concept well-known in the field of psychology. Objects often hold memories and sentimentality, but when given deep thought, many of these objects may no longer serve a purpose or create joy within our lives. Letting go of such items can garner a deeper self-awareness that promotes emotional growth.

Furthermore, Swedish death cleaning is a powerful reminder of the transience of life – reinforcing that one day we will leave our physical bodies behind. This realization can catalyze increased mindfulness and an emphasis on living in the present moment. It encourages us to cease postponing happiness and find fulfillment in the now – to immerse ourselves fully in each experience rather than waiting for some elusive future event or attainment.

The practice extends beyond the individual, reminding us that our loved ones will eventually have to handle worldly belongings. Swedish death cleaning allows us to lighten this burden by carefully curating the leftover objects – ensuring that only items with true sentimental or practical value remain. This act of kindness demonstrates care and consideration for those we leave behind and reinforces the importance of community and human connection.

Swedish death cleaning is an ongoing journey towards mindful living, where decluttering becomes a continuous practice that aligns us with clarity, purpose, and intentionality in all aspects of life. This process is about preparing oneself for the inevitable conclusion of life and celebrating each moment along the way.

As we engage in Swedish death cleaning, we cultivate mindfulness and intentional living by developing gratitude for what enriches our lives while letting go of what no longer serves us. In its essence, this unassuming decluttering method offers us a direct route to a life of inner peace, fulfillment, and connection to our most authentic selves.

So, as we embrace the transformative power of Swedish death cleaning, we embark on a journey towards realizing our highest human potential – living our lives to the fullest with grace, compassion, and wisdom. Ultimately, this practice invites us to contemplate and redefine the very nature of life itself – a timeless process that benefits both the individual and humanity.

THE MANY BENEFITS

In this section, we shall explore the profound influence of Swedish Death on various aspects of our lives. First, we will delve into its impact on relationships, revealing how the inevitability of death can strengthen the bonds among loved ones and forge new connections. Next, we will discuss how embracing this reality can inspire healthier lifestyle choices and a greater appreciation for every moment. Finally, we will examine the concept of legacy and how considering our mortality can guide us in leaving a meaningful and lasting imprint in the world.

Effects On Relationship

This Scandinavian practice encourages individuals to declutter their possessions, promoting a more honest, open, and straightforward life filled with quality over quantity. Here are some of benefits for the relationships of those who practice it.

1. Open Communication: One of the most important aspects of Swedish death cleaning is the focus on open communication within relationships. By discussing one's mortality and openly addressing the process of organizing possessions, individuals are encouraged to be more forthright about their needs and desires. This leads to healthier conversations that strengthen connections between partners, friends, and family.

2. Shared Decision-Making: Individuals can decide who should inherit certain items by engaging in Swedish death cleaning alongside their loved ones. This transparent approach can help prevent misunderstandings and build trust within relationships by ensuring everyone's wishes are considered.

3. Encouraging Gratitude: Decluttering one's possessions allows individuals to appreciate the items they own and their significance in their lives. This gratitude can extend to relationships, as individuals are reminded of how valuable each person is.

4. Reducing Stress: Dealing with a deceased loved one's belongings can overwhelm those left behind. By practicing Swedish death cleaning, individuals can reduce the burden on their surviving family members or friends during an emotionally turbulent time. As a result, less stress is placed on these relationships when they need support the most.

5. Enhancing Empathy: Deliberating over what items to keep and what to let go allows individuals to contemplate the emotions and memories of their possessions. By understanding the sentimental value of objects, people can better empathize with others' feelings toward specific items within their own lives. This deeper level of empathy can lead to more considerate relationships.

6. Building Lasting Memories: Swedish death cleaning encourages creating and preserving lasting memories. As individuals sort through their belongings, they can relive treasured moments and share those stories with their loved ones. Not only does this help to create a legacy that will be cherished by surviving family members or friends, but it also serves as a bonding experience that can enrich relationships.

7. Strengthening Values: Individuals can reflect on their values and principles by participating in Swedish death cleaning. This self-reflection can lead to deliberate choices about who one wishes to associate with, ensuring that relationships align with one's beliefs and priorities.

Ultimately, Swedish death cleaning—though rooted in an acknowledgment of mortality—provides various opportunities for individuals to strengthen and enhance their relationships. By promoting open communication, shared decision-making, gratitude, empathy, and self-reflection, the practice allows people to build closer connections with those around them during their lifetime while leaving a positive impact on their loved ones long after they have passed.

Effects On Lifestyle

This practice has numerous positive effects on lifestyle, often resulting in increased happiness, reduced stress, and an overall more fulfilling existence. This section will explore how implementing Swedish death cleaning can improve our daily lives.

1. Enhancing Mental Well-Being: One key aspect of Swedish death cleaning is the mental whirlwind it generates by encouraging individuals to tackle physical clutter. This process often leads to improved emotional well-being. Through intentional decluttering and organization, we confront emotional attachments associated with items or memories and learn to let go of unimportant things or resentments that might be holding us back.

2. Strengthening Personal Relationships: Swedish death cleaning also impacts our relationships with family and friends. When we prioritize keeping our affairs in order, we are ensuring consideration for their feelings and time, acknowledging that they might one day manage the remnants of our material lives. It prompts conversations about inheritance, personal wishes, and possessions that help create open communication channels and foster connection.

3. Facilitating Mindfulness and Intentional Living: Embracing the ethos of Swedish death cleaning encourages us to cultivate mindfulness about what we invite into our lives. With a stronger focus on prioritizing what truly matters, we become conscious consumers capable of resisting impulsive purchases. Practicing regular inventory of our possessions allows us to determine what aligns with our values and ultimately manifest a more intentional lifestyle.

4. Promoting Organization and Efficiency: The physical act of death cleaning frequently necessitates developing new habits around the organization and daily tasks. Once implemented consistently, these habits contribute to efficiency in various aspects of our lives - from locating important documents quickly to streamlining daily routines by creating designated spaces for items. Such organization results in reduced stress and a heightened sense of control over our environment.

5. Ease of Transition in Life's Stages: By practicing Swedish death cleaning throughout our lives, we prepare ourselves for various transitional periods such as moving, retiring, or elderly care. Maintaining an orderly, well-managed home simplifies significant transitions and minimizes the impact on those around us. This preparation encourages peace of mind for both ourselves and our loved ones.

6. Providing Time and Space for Meaningful Moments: Swedish death cleaning frees time from constant organizing and tidying to focus on experiences and moments that truly matter. With increased control over possessions and the sentimentality attached to them, we permit ourselves to engage more fully in life's cherished experiences.

In conclusion, the beneficial effects of Swedish death cleaning extend far beyond physical organization. This practice invites positive lifestyle transformations by promoting psychological well-being, strengthening relationships, encouraging mindfulness and intentionality, fostering organization and efficiency, easing life transitions, and allowing space for meaningful moments.

Effects On Legacy

The beneficial effects of Swedish death cleaning on legacy arise from a thoughtful and practical perspective that encourages individuals to gift or donate their possessions to those who can truly value them.

One significant benefit of Swedish death cleaning is that it **simplifies the grieving process for loved ones**. Losing someone is an emotionally challenging time and navigating through a lifetime of possessions can add to the emotional turmoil. By sorting out belongings beforehand, individuals can spare their loved ones from deciding what to keep, donate, or discard.

Furthermore, Swedish death cleaning allows individuals to *give their treasured items special consideration* before passing them on. People can create a more poignant narrative about their life by selecting the most significant items and sharing their symbolism. This carefully curated collection will help future generations understand and appreciate the principles that guided their loved one's life.

In addition to creating a richer personal history for family members, Swedish death cleaning *opens up opportunities for charitable contributions*. Many people accumulate items that do not hold any sentimental value but are still useful to others. By systematically organizing possessions and providing guidelines on what should be kept or donated, individuals can contribute positively to their community by donating these items to charities, schools, or other needy organizations.

Moreover, Swedish death cleaning has *mental health benefits* as well. Going through one's belongings triggers reflection upon accomplishments and experiences throughout life. This introspection leads to increased self-awareness and acceptance of mortality, ultimately fostering a deeper gratitude for life experiences, relationships, and personal achievements.

Another significant advantage of Swedish death cleaning is that it helps *consolidate a person's financial legacy*. When individuals clearly understand their possessions, including important documents and financial assets, they can better communicate their final wishes with family members. This transparency helps avoid conflicts among loved ones who might otherwise question or dispute the individual's intentions.

Lastly, Swedish death cleaning *promotes environmental consciousness*. By thoughtfully disposing of items and reducing unnecessary consumption, people can lessen their environmental impact on the planet. This sustainable approach ensures that future generations inherit a cleaner and healthier environment, contributing to their wellbeing and quality of life.

In conclusion, the beneficial effects of Swedish death cleaning on legacy include easing the burden on loved ones during grief, enriching personal history for future generations, providing opportunities for charitable giving, enhancing mental health, securing one's financial legacy, and fostering environmental sustainability. Even though facing mortality can be daunting, adopting the principles of Swedish death cleaning allows individuals to create a more meaningful and intentional legacy to carry on after they're gone.

THE SWEDISH APPROACH TO POSSESSIONS & MORTALITY

In this chapter, we delve into the Swedish approach to possessions and mortality, exploring the deep-rooted connection between our belongings and the inevitability of death. We begin by analyzing how our relationship with belongings is intricately linked to our awareness of mortality, driving impactful decisions on what we choose to own and leave behind. Further, we discuss the role of possessions in life storytelling and legacy creation, highlighting how material items can weave the tapestry of a person's life narrative.

Lastly, we examine the concept of mortality as a driving force in Swedish Death Cleaning, a decluttering process infused with mindfulness and respect for one's finite time on earth. These sub-topics unravel contemporary Swedish culture's complex relationship between possessions and mortality.

ANALYZING OUR RELATIONSHIP WITH BELONGINGS

In an increasingly materialistic world, how we relate to possessions is pertinent. Our relationship with belongings reflects our values, priorities, and mortality. As we continually strive to acquire more possessions, Swedish culture provides a unique perspective on minimizing material possessions in the context of mortality. This approach emphasizes the importance of conscious decision-making, prioritizing meaningful relationships and experiences over material goods, and encourages us to reflect on what truly matters.

By actively considering our mortality when interacting with material possessions, Swedes make choices that prioritize personal well-being over cultural expectations or social status. This awareness fosters an intimate bond between self-identity, purpose, and the items we surround ourselves with – often prioritizing items with practical use or sentimental value as reminders of our values and history.

Focusing on this bond can reveal several ways our belongings mirror our emotional and relational lives. For instance, collectors may find solace in an extensive assortment of items representing their hobbies or interests. Alternatively, some individuals may cherish a select few sentimental objects passed down through generations, connecting them to loved ones who have passed.

The link between our awareness of mortality and decision-making regarding possessions becomes apparent when we consider how contemplating our death influences these choices. By acknowledging that our time on this earth is finite, we can prioritize intangible aspects of our lives - such as developing meaningful connections with others and seeking enriching experiences - over acquiring more material possessions.

In Sweden, minimalism is emphasized as a preferred lifestyle choice. Focusing on functionality and reducing clutter allows one's living space to be more organized, efficient, and serene. The traditional Swedish philosophy of *'lagom,'* which translates roughly to 'just the right amount,' reflects a cultural belief in balance and simplicity in all aspects of life.

One significant aspect of this approach is having fewer but more meaningful connections with the items one possesses. When assessing items for disposal during döstädning, individuals are encouraged to reflect on each item's emotional value. By examining each belonging, we can decide better what to keep, let go, or pass on.

The concept of inheritance also plays a crucial role in Swedish culture around not burdening our loved ones with our possessions after we pass away. The items passed down should be meaningful or sentimental, enhancing their significance and value for subsequent generations. This conscious approach to inheritance ensures that our legacy is more about memories and identities, rather than material goods.

Additionally, the pursuit of meaning in life beyond materialism is evident in Scandinavia's focus on prioritizing well-being and happiness. Scandinavian countries consistently rank highly in global happiness and well-being indexes as they prioritize personal fulfillment and mental health over material gains. This mindset extends to the Swedish approach to possessions, which encourages individuals to garner satisfaction from minimalism and decluttering rather than accumulating material wealth.

Experiences often hold deeper value than physical belongings as they become integral parts of our identity and personal narrative. By recognizing mortality's role in influencing our decisions about what we choose to own and experience, we learn about ourselves and the values we wish to pass on to future generations. With this focus on experiences over possessions, the Swedish approach emphasizes living fully rather than living merely for owning.

In conclusion, analyzing our relationship with possessions in the context of mortality highlights how the Swedish approach promotes a minimalist lifestyle, prioritizes experiences over belongings, and encourages us to acknowledge our finite existence. By incorporating these ideals into our lives, we can better understand what truly matters - from developing meaningful relationships, seeking enriching experiences, and leaving a tangible yet intentional legacy for those left behind after our passing.

Through self-reflection and prioritizing minimalist living principles popularized by Swedish culture, we ultimately confront and embrace our mortality while leaving an impactful statement on what is essential in life.

THE ROLE OF POSSESSIONS

In contemporary culture, there has been a growing interest in understanding the philosophies and lifestyles of Scandinavian countries, particularly Sweden. One of the most intriguing aspects of Swedish culture is its approach to possessions in the context of mortality. How do possessions contribute to a person's life story and legacy creation? By examining the Swedish perspective on possessions, it becomes clear that material items help weave the tapestry of a person's life narrative.

Storytelling is essential to human culture, enabling us to create a sense of identity and place. Throughout history, objects have served as vital elements in these stories, providing context and evoking memories that form the fabric of a person's life. This Swedish approach emphasizes the importance of storytelling in understanding and coming to terms with mortality.

Sweden's cultural roots are deeply intertwined with nature and preservation; a connection that has shaped their societal values regarding possessions. The emphasis on minimalism, functionality, and quality means that Swedes place value on experiences rather than accumulating objects for strictly materialistic purposes. Therefore, when examining one's life story from a Swedish perspective, possessions carry significant weight when effectively serving as mnemonic devices.

One way in which possessions contribute to a Swede's life story is through their inherent storytelling qualities. Objects passed down from generation to generation often come with their narratives – stories of family members who owned the item or cherished memories associated with it. These material items are physical manifestations of memories that may otherwise fade from collective memory.

Additionally, as Swedes gravitate towards high-quality, functional materials, the objects they accumulate throughout their lives tell stories of personal growth and transformation. Items purchased early in one's career or during significant milestones showcase one's metamorphosis over time – reminding us of where we have been and the trajectory we hope to follow.

By sorting their possessions mindfully, individuals can determine which items are most important and worthy of preservation for future generations. These sentimental objects resemble a time capsule or museum exhibit that encapsulates their life story. They offer insights into personal preferences and individual beliefs and values.

Consciously downsizing their material belongings allows individuals to curate the story after their death. It offers an opportunity to reflect on the items that truly hold meaning and are significant in their life narrative. By choosing which objects remain, they actively decide what aspects of their lives they want to pass on as a part of their legacy.

Furthermore, döstädning underscores that our relationship with possessions extends beyond our lives and impacts the stories we leave behind for future generations. Sifting through one's belongings necessitates that individuals weigh the sentimental and historical value of material goods. As such, Swedes recognize that possessions can both shape our memories and safeguard our legacies.

Moreover, when bequeathing possessions after death, Swedes prioritize purchasing functional items first. This ensures that the objects continue providing utility and longevity so that multiple generations may benefit from them. This utilitarian mindset highlights the fluidity of an object's purpose – transforming it from a simple material item into a bridge between generations.

Lastly, examining burial practices within Sweden reveals another facet in how Swedes regard possessions to mortality. Unlike cultures that place vast treasures and items within burial sites for use in the afterlife, Swedes typically practice more modest burials involving only a few personal possessions. This practice reflects their emphasis on the quality of items chosen and belief that only a few key objects help define one's life story and legacy.

In conclusion, the Swedish approach to possessions provides essential insight into how material items contribute to the tapestry of an individual's life narrative. By valuing functional, high-quality items with strong sentimental ties to memories and loved ones, Swedish culture demonstrates how possessions can be transformed into proof of personal growth, continuity across generations, and legacy preservation. With practices like döstädning emphasizing conscious decision-making about material belongings, Swedes have crafted an exceptional philosophy that intertwines possessions with the essence of human life well beyond mortality.

THE DRIVING FORCE

Mortality remains a fundamental and inescapable aspect of the human experience, and how individuals perceive and confront this inevitability greatly influences their actions and decisions. One particularly compelling insight into the impact of mortality on cultural practices is evident in the Swedish tradition of death cleaning.

Understanding the mindset around mortality within the Swedish tradition is key to fully appreciating its rationale. The idea of confronting one's mortality and using it as a motivational factor is not unique to Swedes; however,

Scandinavian cultures generally exhibit a higher tolerance for addressing death more freely than other societies. By openly acknowledging this fact as an essential aspect of life, Swedes seek to alleviate the anxieties and difficulties typically associated with addressing such taboo topics.

At its core, the concept of mortality serves as a driving force behind Swedish death cleaning for several reasons.

Firstly, acknowledging one's mortality inherently prompts reflection on the legacy left after death. In Sweden, it is customary for individuals to begin considering their earthly impact as early as middle age, allowing plenty of time for thorough planning and organization. Embarking on a death cleaning journey encourages people to assess their accumulated objects critically, determining which are worth preserving for future generations or current use, and which can be relinquished or redistributed.

This way, the practice addresses practical concerns and fosters a more profound understanding of one's values, memories, and relationships. By distilling possessions down to their most important components – those that hold sentimental value or practical significance – Swedish death cleaning enables individuals to reaffirm what truly matters to them while simultaneously creating an unburdened legacy for those left behind.

Secondly, death cleaning is driven by an underlying desire to demonstrate love and care for surviving family members by unburdening them from the potentially overwhelming task of processing an entire lifetime's worth of belongings after one's passing. The process can be emotionally challenging for loved ones; confronting sentimental items can evoke strong feelings such as grief over the deceased and difficulty making decisions about possession disposition.

By undertaking this task preemptively, Swedes act compassionate for their loved ones, sparing them the often-arduous sorting process and allowing more time for grieving and closure following loss. The practice also offers a practical benefit; as space in Swedish homes is often premium, death cleaning can help release valuable real estate that unnecessary belongings may otherwise consume.

Moreover, Swedish death cleaning instills a sense of purpose and control amidst the inherent uncertainty of mortality. Confronting death head-on can be intimidating; it sparks existential questions many individuals would prefer to avoid. Adopting the practice of death cleaning offers a sense of empowerment, as individuals actively take steps to prepare for their impermanence and demonstrate self-sufficiency in end-of-life planning.

This proactive approach alleviates mortality-related anxieties and enables individuals to adopt healthier habits. Systematically evaluating one's possessions encourages participants to cultivate a more minimalist lifestyle by curbing excessive consumption and maintaining orderliness within the home. These benefits follow into old age, as individuals are naturally inclined to continue decluttering even after formally undergoing the initial death cleaning process.

Finally, mortality as a driving force in Swedish death cleaning promotes comfort in accepting the end of life as an essential aspect of human existence. Embracing death cleaning compels individuals to confront deeply ingrained fears surrounding loss and impermanence. By facing these anxieties head-on, Swedes are encouraged to develop emotional resilience and a calm acceptance of life's inevitable conclusion.

In conclusion, Swedish death cleaning is significantly influenced by mortality. By acknowledging the temporary nature of life, individuals are pushed to actively prepare for their eventual passing in a manner that demonstrates love and care for surviving family members while maintaining purpose and control. This powerful practice reflects an intriguing relationship between cultural practices and mortality and offers valuable lessons on self-awareness, consumption, and legacies that permeate far beyond the Swedish borders. Indeed, embracing the fundamental concept of mortality can provide meaningful insights into living a fuller, more intentional life.

BOOK II. THE SDC WORKBOOK

INITIATING YOUR JOURNEY

As you embark on this transformative journey, assessing your readiness for Swedish Death Cleaning is crucial. This chapter will help you evaluate your preparedness and clearly envision what lies ahead. Through purposeful and meaningful goal-setting, you will gain the motivation and focus needed to make this transition seamless and gratifying.

Taking cues from Swedish principles, we will guide you in creating a realistic and thoughtful timeline tailored to your unique situation. Navigating this process mindfully ensures that decluttering your space becomes not just a physical act, but an emotional and spiritual journey resulting in lasting fulfillment.

DETERMINING YOUR READINESS

Engaging in Swedish death cleaning can be an emotionally challenging but rewarding endeavor. Before embarking on this journey, it is crucial to determine your readiness for Swedish death cleaning. The following factors can help you assess your preparedness and make informed decisions.

1. Assessing Your Age and Life Stage: The first step is to consider your age. Generally, people are advised to contemplate Swedish Death Cleaning around 50 or older. This does not mean younger individuals cannot engage in the process. Still, those nearing or surpassing middle age may find that their priorities have shifted over time - establishing a greater sense of urgency to revisit accumulated possessions and stories.

Next, evaluate your life stage. Are you an empty-nester whose children have recently moved out? Or perhaps you are recently retired and looking forward to enjoying more leisurely years ahead. Life stages such as these typically signal a transition point – an opportunity to reassess what is truly important in your life.

2. Evaluating Physical Health: Decluttering and reorganizing can be physically demanding. Ensure you possess the necessary strength, stamina, and flexibility to carry out the work involved in Swedish death cleaning. This involves paying close attention to your mobility, strength, and endurance levels. Are you able to lift and carry items without difficulty? Can you bend, reach, and squat during the cleaning process? Determine if you have any physical limitations that might hinder your ability to participate in an extensive decluttering project.

Consult with your healthcare provider to ensure that you are physically up to the task and not placing yourself at risk for further health complications. You may need to enlist the help of family members or hire professional organizers if mobility or other physical limitations exist.

3. Emotional Readiness: Swedish death cleaning involves confronting deep emotions connected to aging, relationships, personal identity, and mortality. Gauge your emotional readiness and mental resilience before committing to this project. It is vital to approach the process with purpose and an open mind to release attachment from material possessions no longer serving you.

Ask yourself: Am I willing to confront sentimentality and release items, even those with deep emotional significance? This self-evaluation will help you understand your emotional readiness for Swedish Death Cleaning. Recognize that, although emotionally difficult, releasing these possessions can provide emotional growth, leading to a more fulfilled life.

4. Time Commitment: Swedish death cleaning should not be rushed; reflect on each item as you sort through possessions in every room of your home. Ensure you have sufficient time to dedicate to this task without feeling overwhelmed. Begin with one room or area and incorporate breaks or periodic rest days.

Remember that initiating Swedish Death Cleaning is a powerful step towards embracing life's impermanence and cherishing present moments. A strong willingness to invest time in this transformative practice ensures that your living space accurately reflects you, leaving loved ones with a clearer understanding of your legacy once you're gone.

5. Support System: A robust support system is crucial for navigating this process. Engage in open conversations with family and friends about your intentions, sharing this journey's practical and emotional aspects. Identify individuals who can provide physical assistance, offer emotional encouragement, or share valuable expertise during the cleaning process. Connect with local resources or online communities for guidance and camaraderie. Strengthening your support network enables you to move forward confidently in your path towards Swedish Death Cleaning, balancing the mindfulness of mortality with the empowering act of creating a clutter-free legacy for future generations.

6. Goal Setting and Planning: Set clear goals and preferences at the onset of this process to avoid confusion and indecisiveness along the way. To start, set clear objectives for your cleaning journey. Consider your current situation, personal circumstances, and the desired outcome of this process.

Next, make a detailed plan that outlines each room or area you want to tackle in your home. Create a timeline or schedule that allows you to work progressively through each space. Equip yourself with the necessary tools, resources, and support to succeed.

7. Financial Considerations: Engaging in Swedish death cleaning may also require addressing legal, financial, and insurance affairs. Ensure your documents are organized, up-to-date, and accessible to the appropriate parties when necessary. Consider designating a trusted individual with power of attorney or executor responsibilities for managing these affairs after your passing. Taking care of these aspects early in the cleaning process will provide peace of mind and protect your loved ones from undue stress during a challenging time.

8. Cultural or Religious Beliefs: Some cultures and religions have specific customs associated with end-of-life decision-making and belongings. Respect these traditions when undertaking Swedish death cleaning to ensure alignment with your belief system or the preferences of your loved ones.

9. Advance Directives: Swedish death cleaning can provide an opportunity to review or create advance directives such as living wills or medical care instructions in case of incapacity. Addressing these preferences during decluttering can offer you and your loved ones more peace of mind.

10. Ongoing Maintenance: Once you've effectively completed Swedish death cleaning, it's crucial to maintain a clean and organized living space moving forward. Establish regular routines for evaluating possessions on an ongoing basis to facilitate a more comfortable transition for both you and those left behind in the future.

By assessing these factors thoroughly, you can determine your readiness for Swedish death cleaning while respecting personal limits during decluttering. Ultimately, successful döstädning leaves individuals feeling unburdened, lightened, and clearer in their intentions for late-life planning.

HOW TO SET PURPOSEFUL AND MEANINGFUL GOALS

Like any other technique, Swedish Death Cleaning is most effective when it has purposeful and meaningful goals. Setting appropriate objectives at various stages of the journey makes it easy to track progress and boosts motivation to continue. This section will discuss how to set meaningful goals for your Swedish Death Cleaning journey, giving you a road map for personal growth and making the process transformative and fulfilling.

1. Understand Your Motivation: To set purposeful and meaningful goals for your Swedish Death Cleaning journey, you must first understand what motivates you. Whether you want to downsize your possessions, simplify your life, or leave a legacy for your loved ones, having a clear reason for embarking on this journey will help you tailor your goals to your unique situation. Consider writing down your motivation and referring to it often to see how far you've come. This will help you focus on the bigger picture and maximize your Swedish Death Cleaning journey.

Example: *Maria wishes to start Swedish Death Cleaning so her children don't have to sort through her belongings when she passes away.*

2. Set Long-term Goals: Once you know why you want to embark on this journey, establish long-term goals that align with your motivations. These goals will help you break down Swedish Death Cleaning into smaller manageable tasks and allow you to focus on the bigger picture. Start by thinking about what you want to achieve in the long term and work backward to determine the intermediate goals you need to set to accomplish those long-term goals. Long-term goals can be as simple as completing one room at a time or making sure that all paperwork is organized, while at the same time ensuring that you focus on the things that will make the most impactful difference.

Example: *After considering her motivations, Maria downsize her possessions by more than half by the end of the year.*

3. Establish Short-term Goals: To complement your long-term goals, you should set short-term goals that are readily achievable. Short-term goals break down the monotony of mundane activities and present speedy fulfillments that boost confidence as such exert consistency in the enthusiasm for the broader variety of tasks. Give some of your selected tasks specific deadlines or break them down into smaller tasks within a specific time frame to monitor progress. Additionally, adopt accountability methods such as tracking charts, alarm reminders, or journaling daily progress, thereby deepening the engagement's effect and frequency of your Swedish Death Cleaning process.

Example: *To meet her ultimate downsizing aim, Maria sets a short-term goal of sorting through and organizing one room in her home every two weeks.*

4. Consider Specific Interests or Passions: As you proceed with your Swedish Death Cleaning journey, you may recognize areas where you're particularly passionate about decluttering or organizing. This can guide you towards deciding what possessions to keep and what to let go of and provide direction for any heirlooms you may have. For example, you may donate a collection of books to a local library or archive if they hold historical or cultural significance in a particular field. Meaningful goals tied to your interests and passions can make Swedish Death Cleaning a more rewarding and personalized experience.

Example: *When Maria realizes she has an impressive collection of vintage postcards, she decides to create a goal around digitizing and cataloging them for future generations.*

5. Reflect on Emotional Connections: Emotions play a significant role in Swedish Death Cleaning, as we often find ourselves attached to physical objects for various personal reasons. Take the time to consider what items hold sentimental value and which ones can potentially bring joy to others once you have passed. Are there any items you want to ensure stay in the family or bequeath to certain people? These questions can guide you in setting goals that align with those emotional connections, making the entire journey rewarding and fulfilling an emotional purpose. Incorporate goals that help manage these emotions while still decluttering effectively. This might include establishing guidelines for keeping sentimental items or working through emotional connections with trusted friends or family members.

Example: Maria recognizes her emotional attachment to her late mother's dresses; she sets a goal to pass them on to someone who will appreciate them instead of keeping them locked away in storage.

6. *Don't Overlook Your Digital Life:* Our physical possessions are not the only things accumulating over time. Our digital lives can become overwhelming, too. Financial documents, photos, and email accounts should all be considered in our Swedish Death Cleaning journey. With technological advancements, apps and programs can now help organize and declutter our digital lives just as we do with our physical space. By considering all aspects of your life, including your digital footprint, you can ensure that your Swedish Death Cleaning journey is complete and fulfilling

Example: As a part of her death cleaning journey, Maria aims to consolidate her digital photographs into organized folders so that her children can easily access their childhood memories.

7. Track Your Progress: To ensure that you are achieving your goals and staying on track with your Swedish Death Cleaning journey, it's important to track your progress regularly. This can be done through various methods such as a journal, spreadsheet, or mobile app. By tracking your progress, you can see how far you've come and identify areas that need improvement. You can also celebrate your successes, motivating you to continue your journey.

__Example:__ Maria keeps a progress journal to record her decluttering efforts, accomplishing her goals, and her emotional journey throughout the process.

To embark on a successful Swedish Death Cleaning journey, begin by understanding your motivations, setting long-term and short-term goals, incorporating your passions and emotional connections, addressing your digital life, and reflecting on your progress. Doing so will make this transformative process more enjoyable, purposeful, and meaningful.

As a result, your Swedish Death Cleaning journey will not just be about decluttering and organizing but also about personal growth. By setting specific and meaningful goals, you create a roadmap for the future while being mindful of your emotional attachments and all the experiences tied to them. Remember to revisit your goals frequently, track your progress, and celebrate small successes to stay motivated.

CREATING A REALISTIC TIMELINE ON SWEDISH PRINCIPLES

The journey of Swedish Death Cleaning requires time, patience, and a realistic timeline to ensure a thorough process resulting in a balanced and clutter-free home. This section will explore Swedish principles that support creating a thoughtful plan for your death cleaning journey, along with examples to guide you through each stage.

1. The Importance of Fika: Make time for rest and reflection.

Fika, the Swedish practice of taking a break with coffee, is an essential part of work-life balance. Integrating Fika breaks into your death cleaning schedule encourages reflective moments crucial to the process. Breaks aid in maintaining perspective and setting priorities, allowing you to reassess your progress.

Example: *Create a weekly plan where every few hours of decluttering are broken up with relaxing Fika breaks, perhaps while shifting between cleaning different sections of your house.*

2. Lagom: Embrace moderation and balance.

Lagom represents the idea of "just right" – neither too little nor too much. In death cleaning, it's essential not to be unnecessarily harsh in letting go of possessions or too lenient in holding onto things.

Example: *Before starting any area, assess the number and types of items present. If a room contains sentimental belongings, allocate more time to make decisions and incorporate additional sessions for when emotions subside.*

3. Nature Therapy: Utilize outdoor spaces and connect with natural surroundings.

Swedes value their connection to nature to rejuvenate body and mind. During your death cleaning journey, reconnect with natural surroundings to maintain mental well-being amidst the tough decisions you'll face.

Example: *Schedule walks or outdoor breaks during afternoons or evenings. These helps clear your mind from the rigors of decluttering and provide relaxation aiding in better decision-making.*

4. Collaborate with Family and Friends: Communicate and share the load.

Swedish Death Cleaning is a collective activity considering everyone's thoughts and concerns. Discuss your death cleaning goals with family members and ensure the process reflects everyone's needs.

Example: Discuss your intentions with children, grandchildren, or friends who might want to help. By involving them, you distribute the emotional burden, gain different perspectives on the sentimental value of items, and pave the way for open communication about cherished belongings.

5. Preserve Important Memories: Remember to treasure what truly matters.

Swedish Death Cleaning doesn't mean giving up all sentimental possessions but rather curating a collection of meaningful items. Ensure you're preserving essential memories in durable formats.

Example: Allocate a dedicated zone for archiving critical memory-laden objects like photo albums or awards, so they stay easily accessible and organized.

6. Be Mindful of Your Impact: Think sustainably.

Sweden has a strong focus on nature preservation and sustainability. During Swedish Death Cleaning, it's important to handle discarded items in an environmentally friendly manner.

Example: Donate unwanted yet usable items to charity, recycle paper waste responsibly, and upcycle old furniture instead of discarding it in landfills.

Creating Your Thoughtful Swedish Death Cleaning Timeline

Now that you understand these core Swedish principles, plan your death cleaning journey by following these steps:

A) Set Goals: Determine overall goals: What parts of your home need attention? Which belongings require decisions? Which rooms must be tackled first?

B) Break It Down: Break down these goals into digestible segments: smaller tasks for each room or category of belongings that can be scaled as needed. Remember to allocate extra time for difficult decisions or sentimental items.

C) Schedule Your Timeline: Establish a flexible timeline based on your available weekly hours or days. Allow adequate time for breaks and outdoor activities alongside decluttering sessions while incorporating the pace that suits you best.

D) Plan Checkpoints & Adjustments: Schedule regular checkpoint meetings with your family, friends, or any involved parties to assess progress and make necessary adjustments to the timeline.

E) Reflect & Adapt: As each room is completed on the schedule, take a moment to reflect on the experience. What worked well? What can be altered to assist future death cleaning sessions? Adjust your timeline and approach as needed for an optimized process.

Integrating Swedish principles into your death cleaning journey creates a realistic, thoughtful plan that ensures a balanced, purposeful endeavor. Remember, Swedish Death Cleaning is not solely about decluttering; it's about cultivating meaningful choices that reflect your life and the legacy you want to leave behind.

By embracing rest and reflection, balance and moderation, connection with nature, collaboration with loved ones, and sustainability, you'll create a plan that helps you achieve your goals while honoring your memories.

THE SWEDISH DEATH CLEANING PROCESS

This chapter takes you through the systematic and compassionate approach of Swedish Death Cleaning. This indispensable guide will empower you to declutter your life and leave a meaningful legacy. Using a room-by-room or category-based method tailored for the Swedish Death Cleaning process, you'll learn unique strategies for sorting, discarding, and organizing items carefully and intentionally.

As we delve into tips for dealing with large, sentimental, or complex items the Swedish way, you'll find effective ways to lighten your belongings while preserving what truly matters.

Finally, let's navigate through the modern-age challenge of digital clutter – sifting through emails, digital files, and online accounts – to ensure your digital footprint is well-organized and respected. Embrace this transformative journey towards simplifying life today and cherishing a lifetime of memories.

A ROOM-BY-ROOM TAILORED APPROACH

As you embark on your Swedish death cleaning journey, a room-by-room or category-based approach can help you methodically declutter your space and distribute possessions with mindfulness and compassion. This section will walk through each room and explore strategies for tackling various categories of belongings efficiently and effectively.

1. Living Room: The living room is where we spend much of our time with family and friends, often accumulating sentimental items that hold memories.

Approach this room with a focus on identifying objects that have outlived their function, such as outdated electronics, old magazines or books, worn-out furniture, and decorative items that are no longer to your taste.

2. Kitchen: Kitchens are notorious for accumulating gadgets, utensils, and cookware that may no longer serve a practical purpose. Assess the contents of your cabinets and drawers while asking yourself if each item is necessary for your current lifestyle. Discard duplicates and donate or gift items you rarely use to create space for essentials.

3. Dining Room: Consider how frequently you use specialized tableware such as fine china or silverware in the dining room. If these items only collect dust in storage, they may be better served by someone who will use and appreciate them. Simplify your entertaining style by choosing versatile dinnerware transitioning seamlessly from casual to formal gatherings.

4. Bedroom: Clothing is often the primary source of clutter in our bedrooms. Use the Swedish death cleaning approach to assess each garment's emotional and practical value – does it fit well? Does it make you feel good? Keep only those pieces that reflect your style preferences or hold deep sentimental value. Remember to also examine other items in your bedroom such as extra bed linens, excessive decorative elements, or personal effects like expired cosmetics and old eyeglasses.

5. Bathroom: In the bathroom, accumulated toiletries, expired medications, and unused grooming tools can create chaos. Dispose of outdated or unused items responsibly, and consider donating gently used products to a local shelter if appropriate. Streamline your grooming routine and personal care supplies by selecting high-quality, multi-purpose products to promote a sense of tranquility and orderliness in your space.

6. Home Office: The home office often becomes a catch-all for paperwork, outdated office supplies, and electronic devices that no longer function.

Organize important documents like birth certificates, marriage licenses, property titles, and tax records into labeled folders or binders. Safely dispose of sensitive documents like old bank statements or medical records by shredding them. Evaluate your office supplies and electronics, discarding obsolete items while updating equipment that enhances productivity and minimizes clutter.

7. Garage or Storage Area: Garages and storage spaces often hold items we hesitate to part with but seldom use. Begin by sorting through tools and equipment—donate duplicates or underutilized items that could benefit someone else. Clear out holiday decorations or seasonal clothing in disrepair or no longer enjoyed. Finally, tackle the sentimental keepsakes stored away - decide whether each item brings joy or serves a purpose in your life moving forward.

8. Sentimental Items: Swedish death cleaning recognizes the personal nature of decluttering emotionally loaded belongings such as family heirlooms, photographs, and memorabilia. Approach these items with mindfulness by reflecting on their emotional impact versus their practical use. Rather than clinging to physical possessions, cherish the memories they represent while determining suitable ways to remember those ties without amassing clutter.

9. Digital Life: Lastly, address your digital legacy: clear out old email accounts, delete irrelevant files from cloud storage platforms, organize photos into efficiently labeled folders, and ensure that loved ones have access to important online accounts after you are gone.

Utilizing a room-by-room or category-based approach tailored to Swedish death cleaning principles will support you in creating a living space that aligns with your values and honors the memories of a meaningful life. You evince compassion and consideration for your loved ones and future generations by intentionally sorting, decluttering, and distributing possessions.

Unique Swedish Strategies for Sorting, Discarding & Organizing Items

As you delve into Swedish Death Cleaning, a crucial aspect to understand is sorting, discarding, and organizing items effectively. This unique process has a distinct touch of Swedish tradition that sets it apart from other decluttering methods. Throughout this section, we will explore strategies tailored to the Swedish Death Cleaning approach, alongside practical examples to help you grasp the concepts.

1. **Sorting items by category:** Like many other organizing methods, the first step in Swedish Death Cleaning is sorting items into categories. This involves dividing your belongings into different groups for easier management.

Example:

- Clothes   - Electronics

- Books   - Sentimental items

- Kitchenware   - Documents and papers

By arranging your belongings this way, you can focus on each category separately, making you more thorough and efficient.

2. **Reflecting on the value of each item:** The key differentiator in Swedish Death Cleaning is the emphasis on evaluating each item's emotional and functional value. Before discarding or keeping an item, consider its significance and usefulness in your daily life.

Example: *A souvenir mug from your trip abroad might spark warm memories of your travel experience. But if it remains unused and takes up valuable space in your cupboard, it's time to let go of it.*

3. Acknowledging the item's impact on loved ones: Another vital aspect of this decluttering process is considering how certain possessions may affect family members or friends once you're not around. Reflect on whether it will serve as a burden or treasure for others and use this as guidance during the sorting phase.

Example: A collection of antique porcelain dolls may hold sentimental value for you but may become a responsibility for those inheriting them. If none of your family members share your enthusiasm for such items, passing them on to other collectors who would appreciate their worth is best.

4. Overcoming emotional attachments: One of the primary objectives of Swedish Death Cleaning is letting go of emotional attachments tied to material possessions. Doing so can create a simplified and organized environment for you and your loved ones.

Example: While some belongings carry sentimental value, not all must be preserved. Old letters and gifts from past relationships may weigh heavy on your emotions; freeing yourself from these burdens as part of decluttering is essential.

5. Documenting your thought process: Keeping a journal or creating a digital document that tracks your decisions regarding each item may be helpful as you declutter. This aids in communicating the rationale behind decisions, making it easier for family and friends to sort through these items.

Example: Write down why you chose to discard or keep an item in a journal entry or digital note for future reference. This could include details about the item's history, its function or value, or your attachment. This documentation can guide those handling your estate in the future.

6. The gift-giving technique: An essential part of Swedish Death Cleaning is redistributing items to those who will appreciate them more. Giving belongings away as gifts helps ensure others will cherish them while clearing out your space.

__Example:__ A box of well-preserved vinyl records may not hold much significance in your life today but might within the life of a record enthusiast friend.

7. Organizing remaining possessions systematically: The final step in undertaking Swedish Death Cleaning is organizing everything you decide to keep in a structured manner. This ensures easy accessibility and seamless maintenance as part of another future decluttering round.

__Example:__ After discarding unnecessary items and giving others away as gifts, arrange remaining clothes by season, color, and usage frequency in your wardrobe. This ensures an organized and visually appealing closet that's easy to maintain.

The Swedish Death Cleaning approach blends sentimental reflection with practicality, ensuring the process is emotionally engaging and efficient in creating a clutter-free environment. By incorporating these techniques and examples into your decluttering journey, you will be well on your way to mastering the art of Swedish Death Cleaning.

TIPS FOR DEALING WITH LARGE, SENTIMENTAL, OR COMPLEX ITEMS

When faced with the overwhelming task of sorting through and cleaning out a lifetime's worth of belongings, it can be difficult to know where to begin. Large, sentimental, or complex items can prove particularly challenging. By adopting the Swedish death cleaning process, you can confidently and easily approach this seemingly immense undertaking. In this section, we will explore a variety of tips for dealing with these unique objects.

TIP #1 Focus on Categories Rather Than Rooms

The Swedish death cleaning emphasizes sorting items by category instead of by room. This approach can make decluttering less overwhelming and more manageable. Start by creating a list of broad categories such as clothing, books, or kitchenware.

Tackle each category one at a time rather than attempting to clean out an entire room simultaneously. This method is especially helpful when dealing with large or complex items spread throughout your home.

TIP #2 Utilize the "Memory Box" Technique

Sentimental belongings can be difficult to part with during the decluttering process. However, the memory box technique allows you to preserve your most cherished memories while maintaining a clean and organized home. Designate one or more small boxes as your "memory boxes." As you sort through your belongings, place any small sentimental items inside these containers.

For example, if you come across an old love letter or a treasured piece of jewelry from your grandmother, place them in your memory box. By containing these sentimental items within a designated space, you strike a balance between preserving precious mementos and preventing clutter.

TIP #3 Take Pictures of Items You Cannot Keep

Some sentimental items are too large or impractical to keep but still hold meaningful memories. In these cases, consider taking photographs of these objects before letting them go. By capturing their image in digital form, you preserve the memories attached to these items without allowing them to crowd your living space.

For instance, if you cannot hold onto an old, bulky heirloom piece of furniture, take a photo highlighting its beauty and craftsmanship. You can then confidently donate, sell, or gift the item knowing that you've retained a piece of its sentimental value.

TIP #4 Dealing with Collections

Consider curating the collection to a more manageable size if you possess many items such as books, figurines, or stamps. Decide on a specific number or percentage of items to keep and commit to letting go of the rest. This exercise can help you focus on the most meaningful pieces while respecting the limits of your physical space.

For example, if you own a substantial collection of cookie jars, retain only your three favorite designs. By curating your collection this way, you maintain its essence while making room for new experiences and belongings.

TIP #5 Consult with Loved Ones

In some cases, the process of Swedish death cleaning benefits from open communication with loved ones. Discussing your intentions and plans for certain belongings can help reduce anxiety, foster understanding, and provide valuable perspective on difficult decisions.

For example, if you have a large collection of family photographs that you're unsure about keeping, consult with your relatives about their preferences. They may offer to inherit specific photo albums or suggest digitizing the images for all family members to access easily.

TIP #6 Make Use of Community Resources

Large or complex items that serve no practical function in your life but remain difficult to discard might find new life in community centers or local organizations. Donating functional items like musical instruments, tools or sports equipment can enable others to enjoy them and sometimes even provide valuable resources for underserved populations.

In conclusion, dealing with large, sentimental or complex items during the Swedish Death Cleaning process can be challenging but not impossible. By focusing on categories, utilizing memory boxes, taking photos, curating collections, communicating with loved ones, and using community resources, you can make the process more manageable while still honoring your memories and making space for a cleaner, more organized life.

DEALING WITH DIGITAL CLUTTER

The Swedish Death Cleaning Process is an effective method to help you tackle both physical and digital clutter in your life, making the process easier for your loved ones when you're no longer around. This section will outline how to address digital clutter, such as emails, digital files, and online accounts, and provide examples of how to put the Swedish Death Cleaning Process into action in your digital life.

Emails are an essential means of communication in today's world. However, they can accumulate quickly and become a source of tremendous clutter. Our email inboxes can become overwhelming with unread messages, spam, or newsletters we never read because we simply lack time.

To begin decluttering your emails using the Swedish Death Cleaning Process, start by dedicating time to sort through your messages. As you do this, you'll notice patterns that will help you identify what emails are essential and which can be discarded.

Example: *Erica is a writer who receives many newsletters from publishers and literary agents. She realized that she hasn't read most of them for years. After identifying which newsletters were valuable to her or sparked joy, she unsubscribed from all others. This allowed her to keep a cleaner inbox and enjoy her favorite content.*

As you continue to examine your email clutter, consider setting up folders or labels to categorize essential messages effectively. Doing so'll declutter and create a system that makes future organizing more manageable.

Digital files are another aspect of our lives that can quickly become troublesome. From photos and videos to documents and downloads from the internet, it's easy for these files to consume valuable space on our devices without us realizing it.

Start by assessing the storage on your devices – laptops or desktop computers, smartphones, tablets – and identify which files are necessary. Depending on your needs and preferences, you can invest in an external hard drive, a cloud storage system, or both to store your essential files accordingly.

Example: Noah is an entrepreneur who downloads several online resources and reports. The process has left him with a cluttered desktop on his laptop. Noah assessed which files he used and which weren't relevant anymore. Then he created folders for crucial business documents and deleted all unnecessary files.

Moving on to **digital photos and videos**, it's important to remember that sometimes less is more. Decluttering your digital memories involves evaluating each image or video, determining its significance, and deleting what isn't essential. This will leave you only with memories that genuinely matter to you.

Example: Mia has multiple photos of her travels over the years. She decided to refine her collection by keeping only images that captured moments of happiness or those she found visually stunning. In doing so, Mia could better appreciate the memories behind each picture instead of getting lost in an endless sea of digital clutter.

Lastly, **online accounts** can become a significant source of digital clutter if not appropriately managed. Assess your memberships, subscriptions, and social media accounts regularly to determine their worth, deleting or unsubscribing what no longer serves your needs or brings joy to your life.

Example: Carlos had several online streaming accounts for movies, music, and sports events. After assessing how often he used them, Carlos recognized that he hardly used two accounts due to time constraints. He decided to unsubscribe from these accounts and only keep the ones he frequently enjoyed.

In conclusion, the Swedish Death Cleaning Process applied to digital clutter can change how we manage our digital footprint while making life simpler for ourselves and our loved ones later on. By effectively dealing with emails, digital files, and online accounts – repeatedly examining their worth before discarding – we are better positioned to appreciate what matters most in our lives without being weighed down by digital clutter.

SUSTAINING A CLUTTER-FREE SPACE

In this chapter, we embark on a journey to sustain a clutter-free space using Swedish techniques to revolutionize our living environment. We build habits inspired by Swedish minimalism, embracing simplicity to create a cozy atmosphere. Next, we focus on mindfully acquiring new items based on Swedish principles, ensuring each addition aligns with our decluttered lifestyle.

Finally, we introduce the concept of conducting a yearly Swedish Death Cleaning reassessment, evaluating and reorganizing our belongings to maintain a harmonious and clutter-free home. These techniques will cultivate a serene space that enriches your life and fosters inner peace.

BUILDING MINIMALIST HABITS

In our fast-paced modern world, we accumulate belongings throughout our lives, leading to cluttered spaces that can reflect a chaotic state of mind. This section will explore techniques inspired by Swedish minimalism to help maintain a clutter-free and peaceful environment while enhancing overall well-being.

1. Begin with an objective evaluation

It starts by stepping back and objectively evaluating your possessions. Visualize the ideal version of your living space, considering factors such as functionality, aesthetics, and mental stimuli. Ask yourself if each item contributes positively to that vision or creates unnecessary visual noise. Preserve those items that hold deep emotional value or serve a practical purpose in your daily life.

For example, for sentimental items, consider displaying them creatively instead of letting them gather dust in a pile. You can showcase a collection of family photographs by framing them and hanging them on a wall, which honors the memories and adds character to your living space. Another way to get creative while being practical is repurposing old items. For instance, you can turn an old ladder into a stunning bookshelf, or an antique colander into a charming indoor herb garden.

2. The five-box method

Sort your possessions into five categories: keep, donate/sell, recycle, discard, and sentimental. This will streamline the decluttering process and provide clear outcomes for each item.

- **Keep:** Items that offer immediate utility or enrich your life. Keeping things that bring functional or emotional value to your life is important. This category includes everyday items used frequently, such as kitchen appliances, clothing, and personal care products. Items with sentimental value, like family heirlooms or photos, also fall into this category. These items will serve a practical purpose and remind of happy memories and positive emotions.

1. **Donate/Sell:** Valuable items which do not meet your needs but could benefit others. Selling valuable belongings can provide financial compensation, making it a more viable option, while donating items ensures that they will be utilized and appreciated by someone in need. Additionally, many nonprofit organizations accept gently-used items as donations, helping those less fortunate and benefiting the environment by reducing waste.

2. **Recycle:** Items unfit for use but contain reusable materials. These items are no longer usable for their intended purpose but can still have value through repurposing. By recycling them, you're reducing waste and encouraging creativity in finding new uses for old items. Some examples include turning

wine bottles into decorative vases or using old t-shirts to make reusable shopping bags. Be creative with these materials, as not only will it help reduce your carbon footprint in the long-term, but it will also open up a new window of solutions in sustainable horizontal thinking.

3. Discard: Broken or unusable items without recyclable components. Discarding these items frees up physical and mental space for possessions that spark joy and enhance your overall well-being. Remembering to regularly evaluate and dispose of unnecessary items will keep your living space organized and in harmony with the guiding principles of Swedish minimalism.

4. Sentimental: Objects with deep emotional significance. As you progress through the five-box method, you may find that decision-making becomes increasingly difficult regarding sentimental items. However, sentimental value varies by person- some items carry deep personal connections, while others may seem trivial. Remember to keep sentimental items that provide happiness and positive emotions, and don't feel guilty in letting go of items that no longer serve any emotional purpose in your life. Stay mindful throughout the process and remember that simplifying your surroundings can offer a fresh start and improve your outlook on life.

3. Replace multi-functionality with simplicity

Opt for versatile items that serve multiple purposes to minimize clutter while allowing flexibility within your home. Evaluate each item's functional use and replace those with duplication by retaining one multifunctional alternative.

4. Embrace digital minimalism

Swap physical books, DVDs, CDs, and paperwork for digital versions when possible. This approach reduces both space consumption and environmental impact. Embrace online platforms, cloud storage, and digital organization systems to maintain order in the virtual world.

5. Regular check-ins and purging

Establish a recurring schedule to assess your belongings and re-evaluate your needs. A monthly or seasonal approach often sparks motivation associated with fresh starts. Use this opportunity to declutter items that no longer serve their purpose or have lost value. Regular purging maintains your clutter-free space without overwhelming our lives.

6. Mindful acquisition

Adopt a thoughtful approach when acquiring items, considering their immediate appeal and how they fit into your overall vision of an optimal living environment. Before purchasing, consider each item's longevity, utility, and potential replacements.

7. Utilize vertical space effectively

Efficient use of vertical space can drastically reduce clutter in tight quarters while promoting accessibility and organization. Install floating shelves, wall-mounted cabinets, or decorative hooks to maintain a streamlined aesthetic while optimizing storage capacity.

8. Develop an eye for simplicity in design

Embrace the spaciousness of minimalist design principles by regularly exposing yourself to art and architecture, enhancing your internal design sense.

9. Celebrate tranquility by incorporating nature

Swedish minimalism encourages biophilic design – incorporating natural elements within indoor spaces. Foster a relationship with nature by bringing plants into your home or using natural materials for furniture or decoration. Such elements promote tranquility and support mental well-being.

10. Establish daily rituals to create new habits

Form daily habits that counterbalance clutter accumulation, such as tidying up surfaces or placing items back in their designated homes immediately after use. Enlist the support of family members or roommates for a collaborative daily ritual to consciously maintain the clutter-free environment collectively.

In conclusion, sustaining a clutter-free living space inspired by Swedish minimalism relies on forming mindful habits linked to regular assessments, selective acquisitions, versatile functionality, and engaging with simplicity in design. By following these principles, you can create a serene environment, experience enhanced mental wellbeing and allow for deeper connections with the people and experiences that truly matter in your life.

MINDFULLY ACQUIRING NEW ITEMS

In the previous sections, we have discussed the importance of decluttering and organizing our spaces using Swedish Death Cleaning methods. Now that we have rid our homes of unnecessary clutter and carefully considered which items truly bring us joy and benefit, we must maintain this new-found harmony in our living environment.

In this part, we'll explore the Swedish approach to mindful acquisition with practical examples that can be applied to everyday life. We'll also discuss how these simple practices contribute to a healthier and more sustainable lifestyle.

1. Closer Scrutiny of Needs vs. Wants: Evaluate whether acquiring a new item is a want or a genuine need. If it improves your quality of life or has a functional purpose, it may be worth bringing into your home or workspace. By carefully evaluating whether each item serves a genuine need, you can avoid accumulating unnecessary and potentially stressful clutter. Implementing mindful acquisition practices can also help you save money and reduce waste by only purchasing what is necessary and useful. Making intentional and mindful choices when acquiring new possessions can create a more balanced and clutter-free life.

Example: *Sara finds a beautiful lamp on sale but realizes she already has sufficient lighting at home. By differentiating between her wants and needs, Sara chooses not to make an impulsive purchase and instead focuses on items that will add value to her life.*

2. Quality Over Quantity: When selecting new purchases, prioritize quality over quantity. Consider investing in items made from long-lasting materials that require minimal maintenance and repair. By choosing high-quality items, you can decrease the need for frequent replacements and reduce clutter over time. In addition to its practical benefits, prioritizing quality over quantity can bring satisfaction and pride in ownership.

Example: *Instead of buying a low-priced set of cookware that will need replacement within a year due to wear and tear, Lena chooses higher-end kitchen utensils made from stainless steel that will last several years.*

3. Embracing Minimalism: A minimalist approach to purchasing encourages us to own fewer belongings and consume less overall. This principle fosters an environment where we focus on items that truly matter while reducing waste and clutter. In embracing minimalism, we learn to let go of the need for excess and instead appreciate the beauty in simplicity. Investing time and energy into our possessions and evaluating whether they serve a genuine purpose can reduce stress and increase our overall well-being.

Example: Elliot has no particular attachment to any mugs in his large collection but understands their functionality through daily use. He carefully selects three well-crafted mugs to keep and donates the rest to a local charity, ultimately creating more space in his home.

4. The Multi-Functional Approach: Consider choosing items that serve multiple purposes or perform dual functions. These versatile objects make more efficient use of available space and eliminate the need for multiple, single-purpose items. Items that serve multiple purposes or perform dual functions like a sofa bed, ottoman with storage, or a vacuum cleaner that doubles as a carpet steamer, can help you make better use of available space in your home or workspace.

Example: Mia finds an ottoman that doubles as a storage container for her living room. This purchase adds aesthetic value and provides additional storage space to help keep her home tidy and clutter-free.

5. Upcycling and Reusing: Consider reusing or upcycling existing objects before purchasing new items. With creativity and resourcefulness, old possessions can be transformed into functional pieces with newfound purpose.

Example: David turns his old ladder into a one-of-a-kind bookshelf, repurposing an old item into something practical and visually appealing. This simple act of upcycling aligns with Swedish principles while being eco-friendly.

6. Seeking Pre-Loved Items: Consider acquiring pre-loved possessions from garage sales or thrift stores instead of purchasing brand-new counterparts. This practice introduces sustainability into our consumption habits, reducing waste and saving money.

__Example:__ Zoe attends a neighborhood garage sale looking for a vintage mirror. She finds one that fits her unique taste for décor and has an interesting history - making the acquisition more meaningful than buying a new piece.

7. Letting Go: Lastly, one key Swedish principle is letting go of items that no longer serve a purpose in our lives. Consider parting ways with duplicate or unnecessary possessions after acquiring new replacements or updates. Doing this, you maintain balance within your space while adopting mindful acquisitions.

__Example:__ After acquiring a new set of sheets, Erik decides to donate his older one to a homeless shelter, putting it to good use while minimizing clutter in his home.

In conclusion, integrating Swedish principles into our acquisition practices fosters mindful consumption while contributing to a clean, organized, and clutter-free environment.

CONDUCTING A YEARLY REASSESSMENT

Imagine, it's been a year since you first embarked on the Swedish Death Cleaning journey as outlined in this insightful guide. With time, you have successfully tidied up your possessions and diligently implemented the death cleaning principles in your life. However, things don't end here. Keeping up with the practices and continuing a yearly reassessment is crucial to ensure your space remains clutter-free and harmonious. This section will guide you through conducting a yearly Swedish death cleaning reassessment and shed light on various examples that showcase the need for routine assessments.

To begin with, let's recap what Swedish death cleaning is all about. Essentially, this practice aims at reducing an individual's unnecessary belongings while ensuring that the objects left behind are cherished and hold value. This holistic process not only simplifies your life but also serves as an effective way to declutter your mind, and make way for inner peace.

The yearly Swedish death cleaning reassessment can be broken down into three straightforward steps:

STEP 1. Reflection

Relax and brew yourself a cup of tea or coffee, as you deeply reflect on the past year's events. This step is essential in understanding how the Swedish death cleaning process has impacted your life. Consider pondering over questions like: Has it brought any changes in your lifestyle? Have you managed to make thoughtful decisions about accumulating new things? How has your home atmosphere changed since then?

For instance, Mrs. Johansson, one of our avid readers, reflected on implementing Swedish death cleaning. She realized how much lighter she felt after sorting through her closet filled with clothes she had not worn for years. Instead of hoarding numerous items, she consciously purchased fewer but more meaningful pieces.

STEP 2. Re-evaluation

Once you have thoroughly contemplated on the changes, it's time to re-evaluate your possessions. Revisit each area or room of your house and critically assess the existing items. You might have surely brought in new objects or received gifts over the year, and it's crucial to decide whether they align with the Swedish death cleaning philosophy.

For example, during his year-end assessment, Mr. Svensson realized that he had acquired several gardening tools but hardly used them on a whim.

Following the death cleaning process, he made it a point to donate these tools to his local community garden, where they could be used.

STEP 3. *Action*

Finally, take decisive actions based on your re-evaluation findings. If you come across objects that no longer serve a purpose or hold sentimental value for you, consider donating, recycling or selling them.

When Mr. and Mrs. Lindberg conducted their yearly reassessment, they discovered a box of old music records stored in their attic that they hadn't touched in years. They decided to have a family gathering and listen to their favorite's records. The ones that no longer ignited emotional attachment were donated or sold online.

Yearly assessments also play a crucial role in ensuring you focus on leaving behind precious memories instead of unwanted possessions for your loved ones. For instance, Ingrid's grandmother Ella was an ardent fan of Swedish death cleaning and passed away last year. She left behind beautiful handcrafted quilts – one for each family member – and a touching note elucidating her feelings towards them.

Remember that conducting a yearly Swedish death cleaning reassessment is about discarding worldly possessions, cherishing memories, and focusing on what genuinely matters. Be kind to yourself while handling this process and help cultivate an atmosphere of gratitude.

In conclusion, yearly Swedish death cleaning reassessments ensure that you adhere to the death cleaning principles and maintain a clutter-free, harmonious living environment. By reflecting on your experiences, re-evaluating your possessions, and taking decisive actions, you can embark on another fulfilling year, transforming your living space and setting the stage for a more peaceful and content life.

BOOK III. THE EMOTIONAL JOURNEY

A DEEP DIVE INTO EMOTIONALITY

In this chapter, we will explore the Swedish approach to dealing with emotional resistance and attachment, helping you overcome the hurdles that may arise. We will delve into handling guilt associated with discarding items, offering guidance on letting go without sacrificing your cherished memories. Lastly, we will discuss celebrating progress mindfully and appreciatively, allowing you to fully embrace the transformative experience of Swedish Death Cleaning while honoring the deeply personal journey it entails.

DEALING WITH ATTACHMENT

Emotional resistance and attachment are two of the most significant factors that hinder individuals from decluttering and reorganizing their lives. In the context of Swedish death cleaning, a practice aimed at making life easier for one's loved ones after passing away, it becomes crucial to address these challenges effectively. The Swedish approach to dealing with emotional resistance and attachment primarily emphasizes open-hearted communication, active reflection, and purposeful letting go.

One of the vital practices in confronting emotional hurdles during the Swedish death cleaning process is *open-hearted communication*. Engaging in non-confrontational discussions with family members or trusted friends who can lend support and understanding is essential to ensure a smooth transition through this period of organizing one's possessions. Conversations about possessions often lead to the uncovering of emotional connections, memories, and meaning behind items. Individuals involved in the Swedish death cleaning process can reinforce their decision-making and effectively challenge their emotional barriers by explaining why an object is worth keeping or parting ways with.

Being honest about emotions surrounding certain objects can be therapeutic during this process. Acknowledging one's feelings does not mean they will be disregarded or belittled; rather, it allows for better understanding of why particular possessions hold sentimental value. As part of the Swedish approach to dealing with attachment, creating an open atmosphere enables everyone involved to let go more easily.

Active reflection is another essential component of navigating emotional attachment during Swedish death cleaning. Encouraging lifelong learning and critical thinking, active reflection involves asking oneself questions such as *"Why do I hold on to this object?"* or *"What purpose does this item serve in my life?"* These questions allow for better comprehension of one's emotions and actions surrounding possessions. Through this evaluation process, individuals are armed with more insights into their motives for holding onto certain belongings.

Moreover, applying active reflection while engaged in Swedish death cleaning can lead to a profound sense of self-awareness. Confronting one's emotions head-on generates personal growth and an opportunity to reevaluate priorities. By practicing active reflection during death cleaning, individuals develop their self-understanding and are better equipped to navigate emotional resistance in other areas of their lives.

The final defining feature of the Swedish approach to dealing with emotional resistance and attachment is *purposeful letting go*. One cannot confront emotional challenges if they refuse to part ways with objects that have weighed them down or hindered progress. Parting with possessions can be challenging; however, it is essential to understand that letting go is not merely about disposing of physical items but also acknowledging the memories and emotions attached to them.

Purposeful letting go involves identifying the core reasons possessions hold emotional importance and determining whether or not these reasons align with one's values, goals, and relationships. This approach may involve staging heartwarming ceremonies such as the symbolic burial of sentimental items or sending well-loved belongings to a new home via donation or gift. Individuals are better equipped to face future emotional challenges by releasing objects with intention and respect.

In conclusion, the Swedish approach to dealing with emotional resistance and attachment in death cleaning embodies open-hearted communication, active reflection, and purposeful letting go. Open communication promotes understanding and support from loved ones involved in the process, while active reflection fosters self-awareness and growth in dealing with emotions surrounding possessions.

Lastly, purposeful letting go encourages individuals to move on from physical clutter and its emotional weight. These methods empower people following Swedish death cleaning to address challenging experiences effectively and make life easier for themselves and their loved ones.

HOW TO HANDLE THE SENSE OF GUILT

As you embark on the journey of Swedish Death Cleaning, undoubtedly, there will be a time when you feel overwhelmed by the tidal wave of guilt that accompanies discarding cherished belongings. You may believe that removing such items signifies disrespect or disregard for their sentimental value or the people who gifted them to you.

This guilt is a natural reaction and plays an essential role in the broader emotional landscape of Swedish Death Cleaning. This section will explore strategies for navigating these complex emotions and finding peace while letting go.

1. Acknowledge and Accept Your Guilt: First and foremost, accept and acknowledge that guilt is an inherent part of decluttering. Permit yourself to experience these feelings without judgment. Remind yourself that letting go is an act of compassion, not betrayal - making space for your future self while alleviating burdens for your loved ones.

For example, you might consider donating or gifting items to a friend or charitable organization that could benefit from them. By reframing the act of discarding as an opportunity to give back to your community, you can shift your focus away from guilt and towards a more positive outcome. Additionally, you may find it helpful to create a ritual or ceremony around the decluttering process, such as lighting a candle or saying a prayer, to help you cope with feelings of loss or sadness. Ultimately, remember that letting go is a process, and taking things one step at a time is okay.

2. Establish Your Emotional Boundaries: Evaluate your belongings with an honest heart, defining clear emotional boundaries that guide your decision-making process. Understand the distinction between useful items and those with sentimental value; consider holding onto heirlooms or things that evoke happy memories while parting ways with unnecessary clutter. Your boundaries should foster a balance between honoring your past and creating space for growth.

3. Reframe Your Mindset Towards Possessions: Removing physical items does not equate to dispensing with memories, emotions, or relationships. Consider redefining what it means to possess something from the perspective of experiences, rather than tangible objects; relating to memories through mental documentation or journaling can prove immensely freeing. For example, you can create a gratitude journal to write about the happy memories of each item you donate or give away. By doing so, you are shifting your focus away from the physical object and onto the experiences and emotions connected.

4. Capture the Essence of Sentimental Items: For sentimental items, consider alternative methods of preserving their memory without retaining the object itself. Take photographs or write a short memoir to document their significance in your life so you can revisit them meaningfully when desired.

5. Identify the True Psychological Roots of Guilt: Is your guilt associated with discarding possessions rooted in attachment, loss, or regret? Recognizing the true cause can help you address underlying emotional concerns directly, rather than unconsciously manifesting them as guilt. For instance, you could struggle to let go of an item because it represents a part of your identity that you're not ready to release. By understanding the true psychological roots of your guilt, you can work through them with more awareness and compassion towards yourself. Remember, the goal of Swedish Death Cleaning is not to erase your past, but rather to curate it - to create a personalized narrative of your life that highlights the things that truly matter.

6. Communicate Your Decisions with Loved Ones: Openly share your decluttering journey with family and friends who might be affected by your decisions. Share your intentions and insights on the practice of Swedish Death Cleaning, emphasizing your desire to ease their emotional burden in the future. Additionally, sharing your journey can serve as a source of inspiration for others struggling with similar challenges around letting go.

7. Give Your Items New Purpose: Donating or repurposing items can alleviate guilt over discarding them; instead of feeling remorse, you can rejoice in giving your belongings new life and value while offering comfort to others. Whether you turn old clothing into rags, create a scrapbook to document memorable moments or donate a seldom-used item to someone who truly needs it, there are countless ways to create new purposes for your possessions. By reimagining the sentimental value associated with an object, you can confront the guilt head on and take a proactive step in decluttering.

8. Seek Support from Others Engaging in The Same Process: Connect with others undergoing a similar transformation and share your experiences. Sharing strategies for managing emotions builds a sense of community and encouragement amidst the tides of change. Recognizing that many others experience the same feelings, that many people find solace in repurposing their items rather than discarding them, can provide immense comfort and perspective at this time.

9. Embrace Forgiveness and Self-Compassion: Forgive yourself for any perceived missteps throughout your decluttering journey, knowing that growth evolves from setbacks. Practice self-compassion—with its emphasis on understanding and kindness—towards yourself as you navigate these emotional waters. Remind yourself that it's normal to have feelings of guilt and sadness during this process, and that experiencing these emotions doesn't diminish the value of your work. When you encounter challenging decisions and feelings of doubt, pause and reflect on how far you've come, rather than chastising yourself for the remaining work. With an attitude of kindness and acceptance towards yourself, you can create a sustainable and fulfilling lifestyle centered around what matters most.

10. Celebrate Your Progress: Acknowledge each milestone in your Swedish Death Cleaning journey, whether small or significant. Appreciate every step taken towards unburdening yourself and honoring the memories embedded within possessions. Take time to revel in the space you've created and opportunities for new beginnings. Lastly, recognize that those spaces you've created will no longer house your old items, but now contain newfound possibilities.

Guilt is a powerful emotion that can easily derail our efforts to declutter when faced with releasing cherished belongings or ones imbued with emotional value. By acknowledging this guilt, setting emotional boundaries, reframing our mindset towards possessions, preserving memories alternatively, and embracing self-compassion—we can successfully navigate this essential facet of Swedish Death Cleaning while simultaneously cultivating inner peace amidst change.

CELEBRATING PROGRESS IN A MINDFUL AND APPRECIATIVE WAY

As you work through sorting items and minimizing possessions, you must recognize your progress and celebrate it mindfully and appreciatively. This reflection allows you to honor your journey while reinforcing the positive habits cultivated in the practice.

By acknowledging achievements, cultivating gratitude, and being mindful of the emotions involved in the process, individuals can enhance their Swedish Death Cleaning experience.

Understanding Mindfulness and Appreciation

Mindfulness is the practice of remaining fully present, focused on the moment without judgment. By incorporating mindfulness into your Swedish Death Cleaning experience, you can more effectively navigate emotions that may arise during decluttering. Additionally, mindfulness involves acknowledging and appreciating each possession's value.

Appreciation means gratitude for past experiences and positive relationships associated with certain items. When combined with mindfulness, appreciation fosters a healthy mindset when deciding what to keep and let go of during your cleaning journey.

Celebrating Progress Mindfully

As you move through the Swedish Death Cleaning process, acknowledging and mindfully celebrating milestones is important. Here are some ways to do this:

1. Acknowledging Achievements: Throughout the Swedish Death Cleaning process, individuals inevitably encounter numerous milestones, both big and small. Whether clearing out a closet or giving away cherished items to friends and family, each achievement is worth noting. Enforcing positive reinforcement by recognizing these accomplishments and treating them as significant forward steps is crucial to cultivate a healthy relationship with oneself and possessions. This practice boosts motivation and allows individuals to build a strong foundation for further growth.

For example, implementing a daily gratitude practice can foster a positive mindset and effectively enhance one's ability to celebrate progress. By journaling about one's success and reflecting on how far they have come, individuals can build a sense of accomplishment and personal pride. It's also important to recognize that the Swedish Death Cleaning process can be emotional, and it's okay to acknowledge these feelings. Practicing mindfulness can help individuals process and healthily navigate emotions, allowing them to appreciate and celebrate progress more meaningfully.

2. Cultivating Gratitude: Embracing gratitude significantly aids one's emotional well-being during Swedish Death Cleaning. Gratitude can be found in various aspects, such as appreciating the usefulness of each possession throughout its lifetimes or expressing thanks when others accept your belongings with joy. Recognizing and cherishing these moments intentionally develops a positive outlook on the process.

Moreover, gratitude can be implemented through affirmations or journaling – writing down the small victories and reflecting on them at the end of each day.

Engaging in this practice can lead to a more profound appreciation for personal growth and make the Swedish Death Cleaning journey more rewarding.

3. Being Mindful of Emotions: Emotions play a significant role in Swedish Death Cleaning, specifically during letting go of material belongings that have sentimental value. It is natural to feel sadness when parting with such items; however, it's important not to suppress these feelings. Instead of avoiding emotions or dwelling on them unhealthily, individuals should acknowledge the emotional attachment yet focus on the positives of moving forward.

One way to practice this is through mindfulness meditation, a technique to observe emotions without judgment or attachment. By understanding that emotions come and go, individuals can develop a more resilient mindset and accept challenging feelings as they arise. Mindfulness ensures space for emotions while simultaneously nurturing a more balanced perspective.

4. Creating Rituals for Celebration: Personal rituals can contribute to tapping into the celebratory aspect of Swedish Death Cleaning's progress. Some individuals find solace in creating rituals around possessions as they pass them on – writing a letter, sharing a photograph, or simply holding a ceremony amongst loved ones for emotional support.

Another powerful practice is self-compassion, which can be particularly helpful during overwhelming emotions. Embracing vulnerability and extending kindness towards oneself at each process stage reinforces progress and ensures self-care remains paramount.

5. Celebration Through Symbolic Actions: Symbolic actions can serve as meaningful celebrations of progress in Swedish Death Cleaning. These actions can take many forms, such as planting a tree in memory of a deceased loved one or renovating a space once cluttered with excess possessions.

Individuals can honor their progress by imbuing these actions with personal meaning while embracing the emotional weight of letting go. Individuals can foster a sense of closure and renewal by engaging in symbolic celebration, providing ample motivation to continue towards a mindful and appreciative future. These symbolic acts solidify the change within while concurrently imbuing life with greater meaning and purpose.

Embracing the Emotional Journey

Swedish Death Cleaning can be emotional as you confront attachments to physical objects. Embrace these feelings by:

1. Permitting yourself to feel: Don't regard emotions as obstacles or negative experiences during your cleaning journey. Instead, acknowledge them as part of your history with the object in question.

2. Seeking support: Reach out to loved ones for encouragement during emotionally challenging moments. A listening ear or words of reassurance can provide comfort and strength.

3. Practicing self-compassion: Swedish Death Cleaning is not a race but a journey to enrich your life by allowing room for simplicity and renewed energy. Be kind to yourself along the way; it's okay if some decisions take longer than others.

In conclusion, Swedish Death Cleaning is an emotional and sentimental process during which celebrating progress mindfully and appreciatively can be beneficial. Cultivating gratitude, practicing mindfulness of emotions, creating personal rituals, and engaging in symbolic actions are effective ways to celebrate milestones. It's important to remember that the process is personal and taking time to make decisions is okay. Embracing the emotional journey of Swedish Death Cleaning ensures that each step towards progress is seen as significant and celebrated accordingly.

With these practices in place, Swedish Death Cleaning provides an uncluttered physical environment and an emotionally enriching experience that supports individuals throughout their lifetimes.

SELF-DISCOVERY AND REFLECTION

In this chapter, we delve into the transformative journey of self-discovery and reflection through the unique practice of Swedish Death Cleaning. We will guide you through unearthing personal narratives hidden within your belongings, as viewed through the lens of this ancient Scandinavian tradition.

We will introduce reflective exercises to help you discover your values and define the legacy you wish to leave behind while decluttering your physical space. By exploring life changes and personal growth that arise during this cleaning process, you will gain a deeper understanding of your true self, ultimately leading to a more meaningful existence.

So, let us embark on this extraordinary adventure towards inner clarity and enlightenment through Swedish Death Cleaning.

UNEARTHING PERSONAL NARRATIVES

As we delve into Swedish Death Cleaning process, we also come across a wealth of personal narratives hidden beneath the surface of the possessions we have collected throughout our lives. These stories are not only an individual's journey but become a way of understanding the intersections of memory, identity, and life experience.

Swedish Death Cleaning involves sorting through one's belongings and deciding what holds genuine value or sentiment, and what can be discarded. This process compels us to examine the intrinsic meaning behind what we have amassed throughout our lives. As these accumulated items are uncovered, they unlock memories that transport us back to pivotal moments.

One notable aspect of Swedish Death Cleaning is preserving meaningful mementos while letting go of unnecessary items that only weigh us down. Through these cherished keepsakes, we begin to unravel our narratives. These tokens – whether family heirlooms, photographs, journals, or souvenirs – hold many stories highlighting our shared human experiences such as love, joy, loss, triumphs, and hardships.

While navigating through this process of unearthing memories, several themes reveal themselves as essential threads in the tapestry of our lives. For example, family plays a significant role in crafting our narrative. An old family album with photographs representing generations provides insight into familial bonds and how family dynamics evolve. It is common for people to hold onto letters and handwritten notes from loved ones – simple pieces of paper enacted as time capsules that spotlight moments of intimacy between family members and friends.

Another theme commonly found woven throughout personal narratives is travel. Whether domestic or international journeys undertaken for leisure or professional purposes, travel creates unforgettable memories of exploration and cultural immersion. Collected postcards, ticket stubs, and other memorabilia are repositories of these globe-trotting adventures. As we sift through these relics and reminisce, we are reminded of travel's profound effect on our worldview and personal narrative.

An individual's growth and learning experiences can also be traced through items collected over time. Academic degrees, certificates, and learning materials symbolize various intellectual and professional development stages that define a person's achievements, contributions to society, and unique skills. As we sort through these materials in the context of Swedish Death Cleaning, we acknowledge our accomplishments and how they have enriched our narratives.

The creative expressions that abound in an individual's life likewise manifest as illustrations of one's journey. Be it through artistic endeavors such as painting, writing, or self-expression. Each art piece is a timestamp marking various moods, phases, and ideological perspectives experienced throughout life. Preserving artwork and similar creations during the death cleaning process ensures their unique artistic voice becomes part of their enduring legacy.

In embracing the practice of Swedish Death Cleaning, recognize that you're not just decluttering your living space or preparing for the inevitability of death: You're engaging in a deeper self-reflection that brings to light the wealth of personal narratives that construct your unique identity. This process is an invaluable opportunity to impart your stories to your loved ones so they can understand your life experiences more intimately. As you unearth these precious memories from objects once hidden away in boxes or disused corners, you allow them to contribute to ongoing conversations with those who remain after you've departed.

Ultimately, by actively reexamining our possessions within the framework of Swedish Death Cleaning, we reveal the personal narratives embedded within them. These seemingly ordinary objects become extraordinary hallmarks representing critical junctures in our lives – illustrating how we have grown and evolved. By unearthing and preserving these stories, we maintain our connection with the past while nourishing future generations who will carry our narratives forward.

How Swedish Death Cleaning Can Help Unearth These Personal Narratives

1. Rediscovering Emotional Attachments through Physical Possessions

As we delve into sorting through our material belongings, it often becomes apparent that these objects hold sentimental value or evoke strong emotions —

be it a long-forgotten photograph, an old letter from a friend or loved one, or a cherished childhood toy. These items serve as touchstones to our past experiences and trigger memories that may have been buried deep within our subconscious.

Swedish death cleaning encourages us to slow down, revisit those emotions attached to these possessions, and evaluate their significance in our lives. Ultimately, this practice assists us in making more conscious decisions about what to cherish and let go of.

2. Unearthing Family Histories

Family heirlooms are often passed down from generation to generation, telling stories of ancestors and treasured family memories through their presence. As we sort through inherited items during the Swedish death cleaning process, we often discover fascinating stories that have shaped our family's history and informed our identity.

Peeling back these layers allows us to gain fresh insights into our roots, uncovering unique character traits or beliefs we may have inherited from our lineage. This deeper understanding of our family history can be profoundly transformative and give us a renewed sense of purpose and belonging.

3. Gaining Insights into Personal Growth and Relationships

By revisiting items from different stages of our lives, Swedish death cleaning offers a window into our evolution. As we examine old diaries, letters, or works of art, we can reflect on past decisions, challenges overcome, and important milestones.

This process also shines a light on our relationships –with ourselves and others – allowing us to delve deeper into their significance, whether the relationship has evolved, remained static or dissolved over time. Recognizing these changes is essential in understanding the overarching narrative of our lives.

4. Acknowledging Regrets and Letting Go

As we undergo the Swedish death cleaning journey, it is natural to encounter objects that evoke feelings of regret or missed opportunities. These items often serve as tangible reminders of paths not taken or dreams left unfulfilled.

Rather than dwelling on the negative, Swedish death cleaning encourages us to embrace these regrets as part of our narrative, recognizing that they have contributed to our growth somehow. By acknowledging these experiences and ultimately letting go of associated possessions, we make space for new opportunities and experiences.

5. Redefining Our Future Narratives

Unearthing personal narratives through Swedish death cleaning ultimately opens space to redefine the stories we wish to tell ourselves moving forward. Once we have confronted our past experiences head-on and let go of belongings that no longer serve us, we create room for new beginnings.

By aligning ourselves with newfound values and setting clear intentions for the kind of life we wish to live from now on, we empower ourselves to author a more purposeful and intentional future.

By reflecting on these personal narratives and removing physical and emotional clutter, we can gain new insights into our identity, relationships, personal growth, and family history while focusing on what truly matters. This empowering approach sets the stage for redefining our narratives and building a more authentic and intentional life.

REFLECTIVE EXERCISES

Decluttering your living space is not only about cleaning and organizing your physical belongings. Rather, it can become a meaningful journey of self-discovery, revealing the most fundamental aspects of who you are through reflecting on values and legacy. Swedish Death Cleaning, based on preparing for one's passing by clearing clutter and sorting through belongings, can be a powerful catalyst for this exploration. The following reflective exercises will guide you in discovering your values and legacy through decluttering.

1. Envision Your Ideal Living Space

Begin by visualizing your perfect living environment, considering the environment that would make you feel at peace and content. Note down the aspects that resonate with you the most – whether that's more open space or specific furnishings with sentimental value. Reflect on why these elements are important to you, and how they align with your values.

2. Review Your Belongings with a Storytelling Mindset

As you sort through your belongings, approach each item as if it tells a story or holds a memory. Ask yourself questions such as:

- What significance does this item have in my life?
- Does it represent an essential part of who I am?
- How does owning this item reflect my values?

Through this exercise, you'll be able to evaluate which items genuinely align with your values and deserve a place in your life.

3. Acknowledge Your Impact on Others

When going through items you no longer need or want, reflect on the people who have received gifts from you or have kept previously owned objects. Recognize that what we give to others can heavily impact their lives and becomes part of our legacy. These objects can profoundly affect the individuals who receive them, and by extension, become part of our legacies.

4. Delve Deeper into Your Values Through Writing

Journaling about your decluttering experience may bring profound insights into your values and aspirations. In addition to documenting items you've chosen to keep or discard, write about the emotions and reflections you've experienced during the process. These writings could be valuable material for future introspection and understanding of your values and legacy.

5. Reflect on Your Life's Key Moments

As you declutter, you may come across objects representing significant moments in your life. Allow yourself to reminisce and reflect on the importance of these events, considering your growth since then. Understanding how your past has shaped you will give you crucial insights into your values and how they influence your present and future legacy.

6. Identify Patterns in Your Belongings

By examining the items you've kept over time, you'll notice patterns reflecting your interests, passions, and priorities. These patterns can serve as valuable clues to better understand what makes you who you are and how they connect with your values.

For example, by recognizing that certain sentimental items, such as family photos or your favorite book, hold great value, you can better understand the importance of preserving certain possessions.

7. Discover Your Undeclared Values

As much as decluttering reveals your known values, it can uncover previously unrecognized or undeclared values. Use these newfound values to inform decisions about belongings, interests, and relationships and ensure they align with your goals. Completing the idea of discovering values, utilizing them knowledgeably will help you lead a more fulfilling life. By incorporating these values into your lifestyle, you can surround yourself with positivity and meaning. Through further reflection, the process could lead you to recognize values which you may be neglecting. Combining the self-knowledge you glean from decluttering with intentional decision-making can transform your life positively.

8. Contemplate on Your Future Legacy

Take a moment to imagine how others might remember you when you're gone. Consider what tangible belongings or intangible influences will remain as part of your legacy. Use this visualization as a guide to continue making choices that reflect your truest self.

9. Engage in Conversations with Loved Ones

Sharing your decluttering experiences with friends or family can foster deeper connections while allowing for valuable feedback on perceived values and legacy.

10. Continuously Re-evaluate Your Values

Remember that self-discovery is an ongoing process; re-evaluation should occur regularly as we evolve. Embrace opportunities for reflection so that Swedish Death Cleaning serves not only as a one-time event but as part of a continuous development.

By engaging in these reflective exercises, decluttering and Swedish Death Cleaning becomes more than tidying up. It transforms into an opportunity for self-discovery, allowing you to uncover your values and legacy while creating an enriching living environment.

EXPLORING LIFE CHANGES

The art of Swedish Death Cleaning is a transformative process that goes beyond mere decluttering. It involves deeply examining one's life, choices, and memories embedded in acquired possessions. In this journey, individuals can delve into their past and gain a profound understanding of who they have become, enabling them to embrace an authentic identity and continue to evolve.

As we embark on this section, exploring life changes and personal growth through the cleaning process, it becomes clear that these two elements are inextricably linked. Let us unravel the rich layers of transformation that can occur as one engages in this reflective and transformative process.

Understanding Life Choices

Swedish Death Cleaning allows individuals to take stock of their life choices by reflecting on their path. It enables them to comprehend why certain items hold meaning, unveiling stories and lessons that may have otherwise been lost.

As one sorts through belongings, each object triggers questions about personal values and priorities. Were they driven by materialism or genuine need? Did these items enrich their life or merely accumulate over time without purpose? By evaluating these choices, individuals can make better decisions and focus on building a life rich with experiences and genuine connections rather than material things.

Building Stronger Relationships

Swedish Death Cleaning encourages conversation with loved ones, providing an opportunity to build stronger relationships. Discussing belongings with family members brings up powerful emotions and exposes vulnerabilities. These conversations allow people to resolve lingering conflicts or misunderstandings, fostering emotional closeness and mutual understanding.

Furthermore, sharing stories about objects with sentimental value strengthens social bonds by celebrating shared memories as a family. This deepening of connections enables individuals to grow into more compassionate and empathetic beings prioritizing love above all else.

Releasing Emotional Baggage

An undeniable element of Swedish Death Cleaning is releasing emotional baggage through letting go of physical possessions. It helps individuals to confront their past, identify areas of unresolved pain and loss, and in turn, allows them to move forward.

As one sorts through possessions that evoke strong emotions, they are forced to confront why these items were held onto for so long. This process of acknowledgment and release can be profoundly cathartic, enabling individuals to unburden themselves and move forward with a renewed sense of purpose and clarity.

Embracing Authenticity

Swedish Death Cleaning promotes authenticity by encouraging individuals to let go of possessions that no longer serve them or reflect their true identity. In evaluating which belongings hold genuine value and meaning, people become acutely aware of their true preferences, desires, and needs.

This newfound self-awareness empowers them to create a life more aligned with their authentic selves. By doing so, they can readily embrace personal growth and transform into the person they aspire to be.

Creating Space for New Experiences

As one declutters their physical space, new opportunities, experiences, hobbies, and relationships can enter their life. Swedish Death Cleaning invites individuals to thoughtfully consider how each possession contributes or detracts from their overall happiness to create an environment that nurtures personal growth and promotes a sense of fulfillment.

Overall, Swedish Death Cleaning is not just about decluttering one's home; it's about digging deep into the crevices of the soul to better understand who we are as individuals. This process provides insight into our lives thus far while opening up space for new possibilities.

By exploring life changes and personal growth through the cleaning process, we allow ourselves to reflect on our past while looking forward with hope and determination for a brighter future – surrounded by genuine connections and experiences that enrich our lives.

ADDRESSING ACCEPTANCE OF LETTING GO

This thought-provoking chapter delves into the profound connection between accepting our mortality and living a life free of clutter. Drawing inspiration from the Swedish perspective on mortality, we examine how embracing the inevitable can guide us in the cathartic cleaning process.

As we deepen our understanding and acceptance of letting go, we reveal the liberating power that decluttering holds in facing our mortality. By casting off the burden of unnecessary possessions, we can live in present harmony and peace.

Finally, we conclude with inspiring reflections on embracing a Swedish-inspired lifestyle that cherishes simplicity and mindfulness - a life lived fully, unencumbered by worldly distractions, and at peace with our brief existence.

THE SWEDISH PERSPECTIVE ON MORTALITY

As we delve into the final chapter of *"The Swedish Death Cleaning Bible,"* it is crucial to explore the unique perspective on mortality inherent in Swedish culture, particularly concerning the practice of death cleaning. At the heart of this process lies the understanding that accepting our ever-present mortality is not morbid but a conscious acknowledgment that allows us to live fuller lives and leave a lighter burden for those we leave behind.

Death cleaning, or 'döstädning,' is a gentle and practical approach that intertwines aspects of minimalism and mindfulness with an acceptance of the inevitability of death. In Sweden, there is a fundamental belief that house cleaning should be an ongoing, lifelong process—a way to preserve cherished memories while discarding items that hold no emotional or functional value. The goal is to create more livable spaces and lighten the load for loved ones who will eventually have to handle one's belongings after death.

One essential aspect of the Swedish perspective on mortality lies in the belief that talking openly about death and acknowledging its inevitability can foster deeper connections with ourselves and others. By normalizing discussions about our finite existence and embracing the reality of our ultimate departure from this world, Swedes believe we can enhance our overall well-being— emotionally, psychologically, and spiritually.

In fact, 'döstädning' can be considered more than just a physical act; it is also a psychological process to establish emotional closure. By reflecting on one's mortality while handling material possessions acquired over a lifetime, individuals are prompted to confront unresolved emotions and life events. This act serves as an opportunity for introspection and growth, allowing people to express their desires concerning their personal belongings, funeral arrangements, and other preferences concerning their post-mortem wishes.

The Swedish approach also emphasizes the importance of considering how our actions will impact those we leave behind. Through 'döstädning,' individuals can simplify the grieving process for their loved ones by removing the burden of sorting through a lifetime of accumulated possessions and allowing them to focus on healing. By doing this, they also subtly remind those left behind that death is an inescapable part of life, encouraging them to confront their mortality and perhaps begin their processes of cleansing and self-reflection.

Death cleaning can also create an opportunity for storytelling and sharing memories with younger generations. As families work together to declutter a home and honor the memory of a deceased loved one, older generations can impart valuable lessons on tradition, family history, and personal legacy. These shared experiences create stronger family bonds and enforce the idea that our possessions represent threads in the fabric of our lives, connecting us with the past and future.

Furthermore, the Swedish approach to mortality involves finding a balance between living for today and preparing for tomorrow. Satisfaction comes from living in harmony with one's environment by maintaining a balance between acquiring items that bring joy and ensuring these items don't overwhelm or hinder one's pursuit of life goals.

Ultimately, the Swedish model for embracing mortality has its roots in practicality, mindfulness, self-reflection, and deep respect for our existence's finite nature and the importance of leaving positive legacies for future generations. By acknowledging death's inevitability at every stage, we can create enriched experiences while shedding material burdens that often hold us back.

By taking this journey through ultimate guide and embracing these principles, one can transform their life by creating a beautiful physical environment and fostering emotional well-being, stronger familial connections, and a renewed appreciation for the preciousness of time.

DEEPENING ACCEPTANCE OF LETTING GO

When we think about letting go, we usually consider releasing our emotional or physical attachments to people, possessions, situations, and beliefs. In the context of Swedish Death Cleaning (SDC), however, letting go takes on a new level of significance.

Understanding Letting Go Through Swedish Death Cleaning

Swedish Death Cleaning is an exercise in understanding and accepting mortality, simplifying our lives, and preparing for the inevitable. The primary goal of this method is to help eliminate unnecessary burdens on our loved ones after we're gone. The holistic approach allows us to reassess our priorities and declutter emotionally, physically, and mentally while refining the legacy we leave behind.

As we engage in each step of SDC, from sorting through personal belongings to organizing important documents, we confront challenging emotions that evoke memories tied to different life stages. Addressing these emotions head-on is essential because denying or avoiding these feelings can hinder us from making progress in completely decluttering ourselves.

Physically clearing space offers an opportunity to confront larger issues that daily stressors may have overshadowed. Letting go isn't limited to discarding material belongings; it encompasses relinquishing negative thoughts, unproductive behaviors, and detrimental habits that no longer support or align with who we are now.

Emotional Acceptance

To deepen our understanding of letting go through SDC, it's helpful to embrace the concept on an emotional level. It requires acknowledging that certain relationships – with people, memories, or objects – may no longer serve our present or future selves. Emotional acceptance is a process wherein:

1. We understand that holding on to outdated beliefs or unresolved emotions can stifle us from achieving personal growth.
2. We recognize our vulnerabilities and make peace with them, freeing ourselves from the past, and embracing personal evolution.
3. We forgive ourselves and others for real or perceived wrongs, fostering inner healing and self-love.

These steps open pathways to spiritual growth and cultivate inner strength when practiced consistently. Emotional acceptance leads to realizing that holding on to emotional baggage can generate resentment or bitterness while allowing forgiveness and compassion as we progress on our SDC journey.

Letting Go of Past Experiences

We frequently encounter situations that leave indelible marks on our psyche. As we work through SDC, we are inevitably reminded of these experiences. Letting go isn't about disregarding or trivializing such events but accepting that they happened, extracting valuable lessons to guide us, and releasing residual negative energy.

Some memories will be more challenging to process than others; allowing time for personal reflection is vital in understanding which events have contributed significantly to our positive and negative development. By addressing these memories in parallel with physical decluttering, we can liberate pent-up emotions and experience real healing on various levels.

The Power of Gratitude

Developing an attitude of gratitude is essential in deepening our understanding and acceptance of letting go during SDC. Gratitude allows us to recognize blessings that empower us to let go of what no longer serves a purpose – emotionally or materially. Daily focusing on positive aspects shifts our energy toward growth, limiting negative emotions tied to the past.

Begin by expressing gratitude for yourself, your experiences, your relationships, your possessions (both current and those you've let go), personal achievements, lessons learned from setbacks, acts of kindness extended or received – whatever feeds your soul. Emphasize the feeling of abundance instead of scarcity; embrace the transformative power that gratitude can bring to your SDC journey.

Letting Go: A Lifelong Journey

SDC is a personal and profound process of self-discovery and growth. Embracing the art of letting go allows us to evolve emotionally, physically, and spiritually. By deepening our understanding and acceptance of letting go through Swedish Death Cleaning—a gentle, systematic approach—we create space and opportunity for continuous reflection and personal improvement.

Remember that SDC isn't an end in itself; it's a lifelong journey that requires honesty, self-reflection, compassion, and commitment. As you navigate this path, regularly revisit the goals you've set for yourself and assess your progress. Stay open and receptive to change, guided by gratitude and emotional acceptance. Remember that letting go is an ongoing process, and making mistakes or stumbling is okay.

Embracing the journey and viewing it as an opportunity for personal growth can help you develop resilience and an unshakeable sense of self. Keep moving forward with SDC, with each step as a reminder that letting go is an act of self-love and empowerment.

THE LIBERATING POWER OF DECLUTTERING

It is essential to acknowledge the inevitable, yet often ignored, reality that faces every individual: mortality. While facing our mortality can be daunting, a unique sense of liberation comes with decluttering and embracing Swedish death cleaning to come to terms with the transience of human life. As the Swedish practice of döstädning, or death cleaning, reveals, releasing stagnant material belongings can result in remarkable clarity within our physical environment, minds, and souls.

In a world consumed with materialism and affluence, it's easy to accumulate possessions that have little intrinsic value or meaning. Heaped in corners of our homes, these items gather dust and weigh us down emotionally with the burden of their presence. They are subtle reminders of missed opportunities, failed relationships, or unrealized dreams. As we confront our mortality, decluttering becomes more than just an exercise in organization; it becomes an opportunity for personal liberation and transcendence.

Decluttering provides a conduit for reevaluating our values, facing our mortality head-on, and realizing what truly matters to us in this transient existence. Here are some aspects that illustrate the liberating power of decluttering in facing our mortality:

1. Acknowledging Impermanence: With each item we release from our grasp during the death cleaning process, we are confronted with the truth that everything is temporary. This practice forces us to acknowledge impermanence – both of material possessions and life itself – teaching us valuable lessons about humility, gratitude, and cherishing those things that matter most.

2. Letting Go of Attachments: Our attachment on material belongings stems from our innate desire for stability and permanence amidst life's uncertainties. However, letting go of these attachments allows us to embrace the fleeting nature of life with open arms. As we accept that objects do not bring lasting happiness or security, we focus on fostering connections, experiences, and memories that nurture our souls.

3. Empathy and Burden Reduction: Death cleaning encourages us to consider how our clutter affects us and those we leave behind. By curating our belongings to make the lives of our loved ones simpler after we pass on, we are reminded of our human interconnectedness, mortality and legacy. This thoughtfulness cultivates empathy for others and concurrently relieves material and emotional burdens.

4. Prioritizing the Truly Valuable: Assessing the worth of our accumulated possessions highlights the fleeting importance of material items in light of our inevitable end. This realization lets us prioritize meaningful relationships, personal growth, and life's intangible riches over material wealth.

5. Emotional Healing Through Decluttering: Many possess items that remind us of past grief, unresolved wounds or unprocessed pain. Confronting these emotions as we declutter can catalyze necessary emotional healing that leads to greater acceptance and ultimately forgiveness – toward ourselves and others.

6. Fearlessly Facing Our Mortality: Undertaking death cleaning exposes the undeniable truth that we will no longer be here one day. This confrontation with our mortality empowers us to reassess our priorities, focus on what truly matters in life, and live each remaining day with a renewed sense of purpose.

7. Culminating Spiritual Growth: The underlying theme in this decluttering journey revolves around spiritual growth achieved through detaching from the material world and embracing the impermanence intrinsic within all things. As we relinquish physical clutter from our lives, we unearth a sense of wholeness that transcends material possessions – a sense that accompanies us beyond this plane.

By surrendering the objects that no longer serve us, we free ourselves from material attachments and uncover deeper layers of meaning, purpose, and liberation that impact our lives well into our final days.

EMBRACING A SWEDISH-INSPIRED LIFESTYLE

As we draw to the close of this enlightening journey, it's crucial to take a moment and reflect on the significant lessons and profound wisdom that embracing a Swedish-inspired lifestyle has offered us. The primary goal of this transformative approach is to address mortality, acceptance, and letting go – concepts we are often unwilling to face head-on but that resonate in every facet of our lives.

In the spirit of döstädning, or the art of Swedish death cleaning, we have discovered a way to declutter and simplify our lives, leaving behind only what truly matters. Through this process, we take charge of our physical space and achieve clarity in our emotional realm. Accepting the certainty of death opens up endless possibilities for living more mindfully and cherishing our time on this earth.

Addressing mortality empowers us to confront other aspects of our life with courage and honesty. This newfound awareness allows us to make deliberate choices about how we want to live while ensuring that we hold onto only what is genuine and meaningful —possessions, relationships, or experiences. By examining our lives through the lens of mortality, we are liberated from the pressures and anxieties that inhibit personal growth.

A key aspect of leading a Swedish-inspired life is cultivating acceptance in all its forms. By embracing vulnerability and accepting the imperfections within ourselves and others, we cultivate empathy — leading to everlasting connections and stronger relationships built on trust and understanding. Simultaneously addressing resentment, bitterness, and past traumas becomes a profoundly important part of fostering acceptance within ourselves.

Letting go is another essential element rooted in Swedish philosophy. Humans often clutch tirelessly at control over our environment and those around us. However, we can relinquish this need by practicing letting go, empowering ourselves to experience life more fully without being held back by unrealized expectations. Additionally, letting go works perfectly with addressing mortality and acceptance, enabling us to release unnecessary burdens, heal unresolved emotional issues, and embrace the naturality of change.

The Swedish-inspired way of living explored in this book is not merely about adopting foreign concepts or making a list of resolutions to start on New Year's Day. It is a lifelong journey designed to empower us in shaping our paths toward fulfillment and significance. Every step towards embracing these principles represents a step closer to inner harmony, profound wisdom, and an undiminished zest for life.

The powerful lessons from this remarkable culture and its people will continue to ripple through our lives long after we turn the final page. The transformative potential of these practises is boundless, spurring positive shifts within ourselves and the world around us. By establishing routines rooted in mindfulness, gratitude, and simplicity, we can craft a satisfying and profound life, leaving behind a legacy worth remembering.

Finally, when it's time for us to exit the stage, having embraced the wisdom offered by Swedish-inspired lifestyle principles will help ensure that we have lived each day with purpose and intention — leaving behind no regrets, teeming with precious memories, cherished relationships, and an unwavering appreciation for all that we experienced during our journey on this planet.

In conclusion, adopting a Swedish-inspired lifestyle offers distinctive tools for contemplating our inevitable end while simultaneously illuminating the path to greater contentment in the present moment. By actively engaging with these time-honored traditions and philosophies— addressing mortality, accepting ourselves and others fully without judgment or prejudice, and learning to let go gracefully— we cultivate more purposeful lives filled with compassion, gratitude, and unshakable tranquility. Such invaluable gifts are worth pursuing — opening ourselves up to fully experiencing all that life has to offer while honoring our inevitable departure with a loving and understanding heart.

CONCLUSION

My dear reader, as we close the last pages of "The Swedish Death Cleaning Bible", we leave you not at an end, but at the brink of a beautiful beginning. Together, we've traversed the tender landscapes of Swedish Death Cleaning, unearthing its roots, embracing its philosophy, and celebrating its profound impact on our homes and souls. Like a journey through a quaint Swedish countryside, we've learned to appreciate the significance of decluttering and reevaluating our relationship with our possessions in light of our mortality.

Through this heartfelt journey, we have found that the clutter in our homes often mirrors the clutter in our hearts. By engaging in this Swedish tradition, we've discovered a more mindful and intentional way of living that enhances our relationships and leaves a legacy imbued with love and care.

We've armed ourselves with practical strategies to embark on our Swedish Death Cleaning voyage. We've learned to honor the sentimental value of our possessions and recognize when it's time to let go. We've tackled the digital deluge, and learned to maintain a serene space through the principles of Swedish minimalism.

Most importantly, dear reader, we have delved deep into what it means to truly live. We've confronted our mortality, unearthed personal narratives, and identified our true values. By letting go of what no longer serves us, we've found an indescribable freedom and created room for what truly matters.

As we step into our future, enriched by these Swedish principles, let us cradle the wisdom and growth encapsulated within these pages. May we continue our journey of decluttering, not only our homes but also our hearts and minds. May we cultivate rich, full lives for ourselves and those who come after us, leaving behind a legacy of love, care, and serene spaces. And may the spirit of

Swedish Death Cleaning guide us towards a life brimming with peace, joy, and mindful living.

All the best,

Linn Sjöberg

Made in the USA
Monee, IL
21 April 2024

57283050R00059